THE
RAILWAYS
OF
TOTTENHAM

UNIFORM IN
THIS SERIES.
EDITED AND
DESIGNED BY
G. H. LAKE

*A History of
the Isle of Man
Railway—Macnab*

*Narrow Gauge
Railways of
Ireland—Fayle*

First Published April, 1945

The sign of a good railway book

LONDON
GREENLAKE PUBLICATIONS LIMITED
Printed by W. P. GRIFFITH & SONS, LTD., LONDON & BEDFORD

THE
RAILWAYS OF TOTTENHAM

A detailed description and historical
survey of their development
compiled by

G. H. LAKE

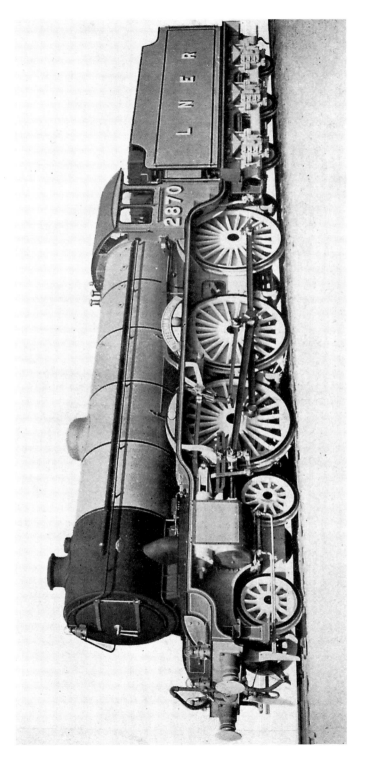

LONDON AND NORTH EASTERN RAILWAY

The original 3-cylinder 4—6—0 locomotive, No. 2870, *Tottenham Hotspur*, of class " B17," which was streamlined in 1937 and renamed *City of London*, and made class "B17/5" for working the "East Anglian" express passenger train.

Official L.N.E.R. Photograph.

EASTERN COUNTIES RAILWAY

CHRISTMAS 1855

An up passenger train passing Tottenham station. On the left is seen a cattle train unloading livestock at the long dock, prior to being driven to the Great Metropolitan Cattle Market, near Holloway. The bridge over the railway is the Ferry Lane highway between Tottenham and Walthamstow.

(From a water colour by James F. Vickery)

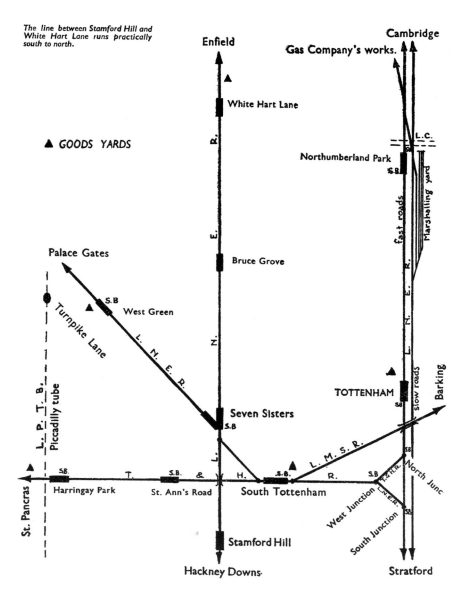

The line between Stamford Hill and White Hart Lane runs practically south to north.

▲ GOODS YARDS

A diagramatic map of the various railways and stations within the Borough of Tottenham.

PREFACE

It has occurred to me that some of my readers may be wondering why I considered that the railways within the Borough of Tottenham are of sufficient interest and importance to warrant my taking some little trouble in research to enable me to compile this separate and detailed record on their account. Actually, I had intended originally to put together a brief article on the subject, but I soon found that the matter was far too complicated for short treatment, and working on the principle that anything worth doing is worth doing in a manner in which one is most capable, I concluded that the only way to do justice to the subject was to extend it to book form, with all the necessary illustrations, line drawings and appendices. After all, the main line through Tottenham is one of the oldest lengths of railway in the country and much of historic interest—from the railway point of view —has happened in connection with it.

Despite the enormous amount of books that have been turned out on the subject of railways, there are remarkably few that can rightly be regarded as standard works of reference, fewer still are the books in full detail dealing with particularly small railways, or groups of railways. Mr. Charles E. Lee has been a pioneer in this field and his three recent books entitled *The Evolution of Railways, The First Passenger Railway* and *Early Railways in Surrey* are excellent examples of authentic and detailed railway histories. Therefore, when I discovered the amount of early history involved in the development of the railways passing through Tottenham I concluded that it might be of some small help to future—and, I modestly hope, present—railway enthusiasts and others, to group all the facts between two covers for permanent record. I was encouraged in this idea by the Borough Librarian, Mr. W. A. Bennett, who is a keen collector of data and matters concerning Tottenham and has a deep personal interest in the locality ; I am indebted to him for placing at my disposal the early files of the local press and other books and maps ; also for the loan of the lantern slide reproduced on page 49. Further encouragement to make this book as comprehensive as possible came from Mr. George Dow, Press Relations Officer, L.N.E.R., who kindly furnished me with many necessary details, documents and facilities for obtaining information at first hand ; also for checking over the text, giving much valuable advice and providing several official photographs reproduced within.

I must also acknowledge the fact that for much of the early history I made reference to the very excellent series of articles that appeared in the *Great Eastern Railway Magazine* under the title " The Predecessors of the Great Eastern," by W. R. Jenkinson, who was that Company's Secretary.

I am much indebted to Mr. T. S. Lascelles who has been at some pains to assist me with matters concerning the signalling and accident details and offering kindly advice in the framing of my account of the several accidents reported in Chapter III.

From Mr. K. A. C. R. Nunn I received a batch of copious notes that contained most interesting details of train working on the Cambridge main line of the late Great Eastern Railway, and from his generosity in providing me with this knowledge I was enabled to formulate Chapter IV into something like a comprehensive review of train working in and around Tottenham. As is well known amongst railway enthusiasts, Mr. Nunn has an extensive knowledge of Great Eastern locomotive matters and I express my gratitude to him for placing it so readily at my disposal.

My thanks are also due to Mr. James F. Vickery, who, apart from providing the original of the colour plate within, also kindly undertook some research work for me and confirmed many details.

I have to thank J. Dickinson & Co., Ltd., for kindly allowing me to reproduce the four excellent pictures of the 1929 accident which took place on the main line at the rear of their Basildon Works, South Tottenham.

Finally, I must acknowledge my grateful thanks to three other gentlemen—the Station-masters at Tottenham, South Tottenham and Seven Sisters, Messrs. A. F. Griggs, S. Curtis and C. Gibbins respectively, who were always ready to assist with information and to verify details whenever possible. Their kindly assistance and interest certainly helped to make the task of gathering data for this book a most pleasant one. I would like to put on record here that it has always been my experience that Station-masters as a whole are a most helpful and courteous body of men and my contacts at Tottenham have proved no exception to the rule. Mr. Griggs retired from active railway service at the end of 1944 and I take this opportunity to wish him a long and happy retirement.

London, 1945.   G. H. LAKE.

INDEX

THE
RAILWAYS OF TOTTENHAM

Introduction

HISTORICALLY, the railways passing through Tottenham are more than usually interesting and their story commences as far back as the year 1836 ; strategically, they are of considerable importance and their present development is the outcome of many proposals, schemes and amalgamations. It is reasonable to anticipate that in the future they may well play an important part in the full development of an electrified suburban railway system for the East Middlesex area.

Tottenham comprises an area of slightly over three thousand acres and can boast a total length of surface railways of just over eight miles ; approximately one and three-quarter miles are four tracked, the remainder being double tracked ; there are seven junctions, four goods depôts, one marshalling yard and eight passenger stations, or nine if the now closed St. Ann's Road station is included. About one-quarter of Stamford Hill station is within the Borough boundary and almost exactly one mile of the Piccadilly tube passes under the Harringay side of the Borough, with Turnpike Lane station in the north-west corner.

Tottenham has developed from a small hamlet of a few scattered houses situated between the High Cross and the Hale at the time of the railway's coming, to the present closely built London suburb of some 142,000 inhabitants (1939 figures) and it is now one of the largest and most populous places in the County of Middlesex. Industrial growth has been considerable since the termination of the first world war, and there is no doubt that the very fine steam services that were operated by the late Great Eastern and Midland Railways, and their successors the London and North Eastern and London, Midland and Scottish Railways, influenced considerably the development of the district. Cheap and convenient trains were, and still are, available to the City, West End, Leyton and Barking, Stratford, the Thames Docks and Woolwich Ferry, Edmonton, Enfield, Hertford, and Wood Green. Improvement in road transport communications, especially those provided by the introduction of the trolley-buses over the Ferry Lane to Walthamstow, has naturally negatived some of the advantages of the rail routes, but the geographical position of the railways and their connections are such that the modernisation and electrification of the lines will undoubtedly bring renewed prosperity and convenience as can only be provided by an intensive and reliable electric rail service.

It is hoped, therefore, that the matter which follows will not only be of interest to all railway minded people, but also to those residents of Tottenham who are sufficiently interested and enthusiastic about their home town to read about and enquire into its history, transport, social habits, and general development.

CHAPTER I General History

I T WAS on the 15th September, 1840, that the Northern and Eastern Railway opened its line for traffic between Stratford and Broxbourne for public use. This railway, passing as it does through the eastern edge of Tottenham, was provided with two stations to serve the district. It must be remembered that at the time of the opening of the new railway Tottenham was only a small place, centred around the High Cross, with scattered residences along the High Road towards Edmonton. The main village was served by the station opened at the Hale on the Ferry Lane and was named Tottenham, whilst the northern part of the district was provided for by the station opened at Northumberland Park on the Marsh Lane. This was first called Marsh Lane, but was soon altered to the single word Park, but in recent years it has been known as Northumberland Park after the district in which it is situated.

When first opened the Northern and Eastern was a short railway of only 15¼ miles in extent, but it was the first practical result of a grandiose scheme for a trunk railway from Islington in London to York, by way of Cambridge, Peterborough and Lincoln, but when the Royal Assent was given to their Bill on the 4th July, 1836, the Northern and Eastern Railway Company found that their powers were limited to the construction of a railway only fifty-three miles in length from London to Cambridge. Even this much reduced plan had to be curtailed still further and the Company had to apply to Parliament for additional Acts in 1839 and 1840 for the abandonment of the line north of Bishops Stortford and for a deviation at the London end. The latter alteration allowed for the railway to proceed straight down the Lea Valley to Stratford instead of Islington, the deviation starting at Tottenham. Financial difficulties appear to have been the main cause of these changes, and in the case of the London end deviation it is obvious that the line as originally planned to run under the Clapton terrace, and the closely built district of Islington, would have entailed heavy and expensive engineering work and a large outlay for the purchase of the necessary land. The engineer appointed for the construction of the railway was Robert Stephenson (son of the famous George).

By making contact with the Eastern Counties Railway at Stratford the Directors of the Northern and Eastern no doubt anticipated a cheap and easy method of obtaining access to the City by means of running powers over the lines of the former into their terminus at Shoreditch, but any hopes that they entertained in this direction were doomed to speedy disappointment ; their approach to the directors of the Eastern Counties for permission to run into the Shoreditch terminus was, in the first instance, met with a blank refusal. The Eastern Counties, however, had found that the cost of their line at the London end had worked out very expensively and with their somewhat declining fortunes they were afterwards willing to come to terms with their neighbours. These terms, although now appearing to be somewhat severe, were apparently mutually satisfactory, and the Northern and Eastern were called upon to pay an annual rental of £7,000, plus a toll of fourpence per passenger. Whilst this arrangement enabled the Northern and Eastern trains to run through to Shoreditch and thus save the inconvenience of passengers changing trains at Stratford, it nevertheless had the undesirable effect of causing high fares. This, in conjunction with the circuitous route from Tottenham to Shoreditch—eight miles by rail as against four by road—naturally did not encourage passenger traffic, and so we find that even so long ago the railway found itself competing with the road. Therefore, although Tottenham, and its northern neighbour Edmonton, had the distinction of railway facilities ten years after the opening of the Liverpool and Manchester Railway in 1830, they did not benefit to any real extent excepting for journeys up and down the Lea Valley. In passing, it is interesting to note that the Liverpool and Manchester Railway was opened exactly ten years, 15th September, 1830, before the opening of the Northern and Eastern.

As far as Tottenham is concerned the period 1840/60 is a very interesting one in railway history, and many schemes were put forward, which, had they matured, would undoubtedly have affected the ultimate development of the district, and it is fairly certain that its appearance, and general layout, would be somewhat different from that of to-day.

The Directors of the Northern and Eastern had adopted a " take or leave it " attitude towards their customers and no real attempt was ever made to attract traffic or to operate the line on the idea of its being a public utility undertaking. The position soon became so unsatisfactory that the proprietors began to clamour for an overhaul of affairs, the agitation resulting in a committee of shareholders being set up to deal with the trouble and this in turn resulted in a drastic comb out of the directorate and a consequent improvement of the situation.

In 1843, negotiations were commenced between the Northern and Eastern and the Eastern Counties companies for the latter to lease the line and take over its working, and on 25th October, 1843, a joint meeting of shareholders of the two companies was held to discuss the matter. A settlement was duly arrived at, the main terms being that the Eastern Counties would pay interest at the rate of 5 per cent. per annum on the Northern and Eastern capital, guaranteed not to exceed £970,000, but probably not more than £950,000, plus a certain division of surplus profits. The working of the line by the Eastern Counties commenced on 1st January, 1844, but the owning company did not relinquish all control of their property, as the lease provided for six of their directors to sit on the newly constituted joint board. As a point of interest it should be mentioned here that by this time the Northern and Eastern had succeeded in laying its tracks as far down as Bishops Stortford (opened for through traffic on 16th May, 1842) and also to Ware and Hertford by means of the branch line from Broxbourne (opened for traffic on 31st October, 1843). Tottenham folk were then able to enjoy rail facilities to these important market centres.

Another event took place during 1844 which is of interest to students of railway history. This was the decision of the Eastern Counties directors to relay their tracks to the standard gauge of 4 ft. $8\frac{1}{2}$ in. The original gauge of the railways, both Northern and Eastern and Eastern Counties, had been 5 ft. 0 in., and provision had actually been made for the conversion to the broad gauge of the Great Western, 7 ft. $0\frac{1}{4}$ in., but Robert Stephenson and John Braithwaite presented a report that decided against the adoption of the broad gauge. The work of actual conversion was carried out between 5th September and 7th October, 1844, and this necessitated alterations to all the rolling stock and locomotives. Advantage seems to have been taken of these alterations to change the colour scheme for the carriages from blue to green, and at the same time the staff uniforms were similarly altered.

The Railway Regulation Act, 1844, had the effect of introducing the one penny per mile third-class parliamentary trains, and this with the combined improvement of the working of the line, had its immediate benefits for the people of Tottenham. It is recorded that the traffic receipts of the Northern and Eastern section increased by as much as 32 per cent. in the first seven weeks of 1844 as compared with the corresponding period of 1843, and this before the new working arrangements had scarcely been allowed time to function smoothly. Despite these improvements, however, there still remained the disadvantage of the roundabout journey to Shoreditch via Stratford.

Reference must now be made to some of the abortive schemes which concerned Tottenham. Probably the most important of these was the proposal, during 1846, for a railway to Farringdon Road (Guilford Street* was also mentioned as a possible site for the terminus of this line) to give the Eastern Counties a terminus adjacent to the West End, but the railway of $5\frac{1}{2}$ miles was estimated to cost about $1\frac{1}{2}$ millions, which was considered to be excessive (the same reason for the abandonment of the original Northern and Eastern approach to Islington). The Royal Commissioners held the view that the railway should terminate on the north side of the City Road, but the proposal failed before the Commons Committee. George Hudson, chairman of the Eastern Counties, gave evidence before this Committee stressing the great inconvenience of the existing Shoreditch terminus and the extended journey via Stratford.

In February, 1846, a scheme was proposed for a railway from Tottenham to Barnet ; this apparently was put forward with the chief idea of developing a suburban system, but it failed to pass standing orders, and it was left to the Great Northern to give Barnet the benefit of a railway.

The existing main line passing through Tottenham might very well have become part of a trunk line to Scotland, but it was destined to be otherwise. It certainly would have been a trunk line had the great George Hudson—the Railway King—been able to have had his own way. When he joined the board of the Eastern Counties in 1845 he was already chairman of several other important railway companies in the Midlands and the north of England, one of the most important being the Midland Railway, and there appears to be little doubt that he had visions of the Eastern Counties being linked to the Midland and thus establishing a great trunk road to the north from London. During this period the London and York was being projected and George Hudson and the Eastern Counties company raised every possible objection to it, but all their efforts were of no avail, and on 26th June, 1846, the Bill for the construction of the Great Northern Railway (the name having been changed from London and York) was passed, and this was the end of any hopes which Tottenham residents may have entertained for their railway to carry Scotch expresses.

One scheme which Hudson put forward as an offset to the proposal for the Great Northern, was the idea of extending the Hertford Branch of the Eastern Counties to Hitchin and Bedford, and in a circular the directors naively suggested that this line would obviously become *the* trunk road to London in connection with any railway from the north or north-west of England which might later be built. After the Great Northern company started construction of their line, the Midland Railway obtained sanction to build a line down to Hitchin by way of Bedford, but the Act

*Until about the middle of the last century the spelling of this street name was Guildford.

contained a clause that the Midland line was to terminate with a junction on the Great Northern on the west side of that line, and which it was not allowed to cross. A further and definite proposal for the extension of the Eastern Counties from Hertford to Hitchin was rejected, and once again Hudson's grand scheme to link the Eastern Counties with his Midland and Northern companies was thwarted. Before leaving this phase of the story it is interesting to note that many years later the Great Eastern Railway did obtain a direct line to York from Stratford. This came about by the opening of the Great Northern and Great Eastern Joint Railway from March to Doncaster in 1882, but the use of the through route by the Great Eastern was mainly confined to freight traffic, the chief expresses using the joint line being concerned more with East Anglian towns than London.

After the Great Northern became an established reality it was only natural that several independent schemes should be projected to form a connecting link between the two main lines. One plan, which was placed before the inhabitants of Tottenham at a meeting on 17th August, 1860, continued alternative routes between Tottenham and Hornsey. One railway was to branch off the main line at the Hale station and proceed in a south-westerly direction, passing under the High Road near the Page Green, then under Seven Sisters Road and over Hanger Lane (now St. Ann's Road), and then over the Green Lanes to join the Great Northern at Harringay. This appears a rather odd proposal as to pass under the Seven Sisters Road and over St. Ann's Road, would need a very severe gradient to meet the difference in the two levels. The alternative was for a line to leave the Hale in the north-westerly direction to pass over the High Road at a point near the Ship Inn by means of a wrought-iron bridge, 16 ft. above the roadway ; thence by way of Mount Pleasant and West Green and so over the Green Lanes somewhere near the Turnpike Lane on to Hornsey, where it would join up with the Great Northern. The complete scheme was for the railways to run on to Highgate, Kentish Town and the western suburbs of London, and the proposed title was " North Metropolitan Junction Railway."

Another scheme to link up the two main lines was put forward in July, 1860, with a proposed capital of £35,000. A note in the *Tottenham and Edmonton Advertiser* for July, 1860, informed its readers that " The character of the localities traversed by the proposed lines is essentially picturesque—at present almost entirely open— capable of considerable improvement and especially eligible for building purposes." In the light of present-day conditions of the district, the words " capable of con- siderable improvement " would appear to be somewhat debatable, and it is certain that if any picturesqueness did exist in the scenery, it has long since disappeared.

Another connecting railway was proposed which had the complicated title of " North Eastern and South Western Junction Railway " and this was to have crossed over the High Road at a point near the Pound Almshouses. In December, 1861, still another scheme was suggested to provide a railway between Tottenham and Hornsey but as in the case of the other three proposals it was eventually withdrawn.

At the end of the year 1861, an interesting proposal was put forward to build a railway from Edmonton Junction (presumably Angel Road) to Kingsland Road station (Dalston) on the North London Railway and this was intended to give the Eastern Counties access to the Broad Street terminus of the North London line by virtue of running powers over that railway between Dalston and the City. This line was to follow a route across Northumberland Park, thence at the back of the houses on the east side of the High Road, up under Clapton Terrace, and so to Dalston. This proposal came to naught, but was followed up by a modified version for a line from Tottenham Station to Kingsland Road station. This was projected by the Eastern Counties about March, 1862, together with a Bill for a short branch line to run from Angel Road, Edmonton, to terminate at Tottenham. The position of the terminus was not specified. Neither of these proposals matured, and in the case of the branch line from Edmonton it is difficult to see to what extent it would have been beneficial to Tottenham, excepting for journeys going northwards. Passengers bound for the City could hardly be expected to travel nearly two miles in the wrong direction as well as having to go via Stratford.

Two years later, in 1864, another railway was proposed from the Kingsland Road station on the North London line, this time to run straight down to Tottenham, parallel to the main highway ; this proposal came from the North London company, and it is perhaps just as well that the scheme did not mature as the cheap and intensive omnibus and tramway competition which would have developed early in the present century would undoubtedly have affected traffic adversely. This was proved by the Great Eastern's loop line from Lower Edmonton to Cheshunt, via Churchbury. The laying down of the electric tramway to Waltham Cross soon made itself felt and the line had to be closed to passenger traffic in 1909 (except for a short revival with an auto-train service during the 1914–18 war).

Another Bill which did not survive its passage through the House of Lords early in 1863, was for a railway to run from Edmonton to Finsbury Circus near the City ; this line would have passed through Tottenham.

Yet another connecting link between the two main lines was proposed. This was for a railway to run from the Tottenham station to a point near the Seven Sisters Road station (now known as Finsbury Park). It is interesting to note that in nearly all the proposals to link up the Eastern Counties with the Great Northern it was stressed by the promoters that the herds of cattle which had to be driven over the public highway from the Tottenham station to the Cattle Market at Holloway, constituted a public menace, and that the provision of a railway would be the means of removing the danger and inconvenience, quite apart from the advantage of a more speedy delivery of the cattle to the market.

Before passing on to the next phase of Tottenham's railway history we must make mention of a rather interesting note which appeared in the *Tottenham and Edmonton Advertiser* for October, 1862. This was to the effect that when the new Metropolitan Railway was available for traffic it was proposed to run an omnibus service from Tottenham High Road to Wood Green station on the Great Northern main line, and thus open up a new route to the City—'bus to Wood Green, train to King's Cross and Underground to Farringdon Road. This roundabout journey was to be accomplished in the remarkably short space of time of forty minutes ! Further, the Local Board of Health of the time was prepared to light the Station Road, Wood Green, for the " benefit and safety of passengers."

On 7th August, 1862, the Act constituting the formation of the Great Eastern Railway received the Royal Assent, although the amalgamation had actually been in effect since 1st July previously. By virtue of the lease between the Eastern Counties and the Northern and Eastern, the working of the Tottenham main line passed into the hands of the newly constituted company, but curiously enough, the Northern and Eastern remained an independent company until as late as 1902, forty years afterwards, when it was finally merged into the Great Eastern system by Act of Parliament.

The next important development of the Tottenham railways was the passing of the Tottenham and Hampstead Junction Railway Act, which took place on 28th July, 1862, but for various reasons the traffic did not commence running over it until almost six years later—21st July, 1868. This railway was the first tangible result of the many schemes and proposals for the linking of the Tottenham main line with the western districts of London, but in this case no effort was made to connect with the Great Northern which line it passes under at Harringay. A link was made some years later just beyond the bridge under the Great Northern, but the actual junction with that line was not put in. However, it would have been of little use for trains from the Tottenham direction as they would not have been able to use it without reversing, as the junction with the Tottenham and Hampstead tracks faces in the westerly direction. This partial connection was removed in 1885 and replaced again, complete, during the first world war, removed again soon afterwards, and again replaced during the second world war, this time complete with full signalling.

The Tottenham and Hampstead Junction Railway commenced at its junction with the Great Eastern twenty-four chains south of Tottenham station ; this is now known as the North Junction. It passes through the south of the Borough in an almost due westerly direction to enter into Hornsey soon after crossing over the Green Lanes at Harringay. This railway was destined to become a very important link in London's railway system, connecting as it does all the lines of the London, Midland and Scottish

Railway with the eastern section of the London and North Eastern Railway and the Tilbury and Southend section of the L.M.S.R., quite apart from the important London docks and wharves.

At a meeting of the Norfolk Railway Company held in June, 1862, certain Bills were submitted to parliament, which included one for the amalgamation of the Eastern Counties, Eastern Union, and Norfolk Railways into the Great Eastern, and also for a Bill for the incorporation of the Tottenham and Hampstead Junction Railway. The chairman declared at the close of the meeting that the Bills were agreed to and said that the Tottenham and Hampstead Bill was an important one, and that the united companies would work the line at 46 per cent. of the receipts.

According to the *Tottenham and Edmonton Advertiser* for February, 1863, the first ordinary general meeting of the company was advertised to be held on 27th January, 1863, but for some unexplained reason nobody appears to have turned up, directors or shareholders. However, they seem to have shown more interest later on as several new schemes were projected by the company and although they did not actually concern Tottenham itself, they might very well have affected the ultimate development of the place. One proposal was for a link from Highgate to connect with the Metropolitan Railway at Gower Street (now Euston Square) Station ; this branch was estimated to cost some £400,000 to construct. The directors also toyed with the idea of running a branch line up to the Alexandra Palace, which building was then in the course of construction, and they went so far as to instruct surveyors to report as to the best way to approach the hill.

As already mentioned the railway was six years in the making, and when opened extended from the North Junction (Tottenham) to Highgate Road, but at that time no stations were opened in the Tottenham area as the district was then entirely rural, excepting for the village itself. The first service of trains was operated from Fenchurch Street to Highgate Road, but ceased to run early in 1870 as will be seen from the next paragraph. These early services suffered from the necessity of the trains reversing at Tottenham station, and to overcome this drawback the south-west curve was built, thus forming the South and West Junctions. The hitherto unopened section to Gospel Oak station (a single platform affair situated behind the L.N.W.R. station of the same name) was opened on 4th June, 1888, and Great Eastern trains were extended thereto. These trains had commenced to run in the summer of 1885 between Chingford and Highgate Road, and they were very useful to Tottenham residents, enabling them to reach either Epping Forest or Hampstead Heath with equal ease.

The company was soon in financial trouble and on 31st January, 1870, the Great Eastern respectfully declined to continue to work the line any longer for passenger traffic. A note in the *Tottenham and Edmonton Advertiser* dated May, 1869, stated that the receipts for the five months from 31st July, 1868, to the following 31st December, were £1,271, whilst expenditure for the maintenance of traffic was £1,329, a deficit of £58.

However, early in 1870, and soon after the Great Eastern ceased working the line, the Midland decided to try their luck with it, and on 1st July, 1870, they commenced to run a service of trains from Moorgate Street to Crouch Hill (the Kentish Town connection having been opened on 3rd January, 1870). By this time the Midland had obtained running powers for their goods trains to operate to Poplar and other points in dockland, and as a kind of *quid pro quo* at the same time the Great Eastern obtained running powers into St. Pancras which had the effect of providing them with a west-end terminus, and their trains started running on 1st July, 1870 also. These new services were not really a great help to Tottenham, and in the local press for November, 1870, can be found a note to the effect that application had been made by Tottenham residents to the Midland company to extend their train service from Crouch Hill to Tottenham station, but the company replied that owing to the lack of siding accommodation at that station it was not practicable to do so. The Midland had apparently approached the Great Eastern on the subject but had received no reply. The local paper pointed out that the Great Eastern were taking a long while to construct their Hackney Downs—Edmonton railway, and in view of the fact that Tottenham did not oppose the Great Eastern's opposition to the North London company's direct line (see page 15), they considered that the Great Eastern should act with some grace in complying with the request of the Midland. It was also suggested that the Midland trains should run through to Hertford and Enfield (via Angel Road). As nothing matured in this direction a station was eventually opened at South Tottenham at the foot of Stamford Hill on the High Road ; the 1st May, 1871, was the opening date of this station and the Moorgate Street trains were extended thereto from Crouch Hill. A copy of the time-table dated 1st July, 1871, is reproduced. Excursion trains were also run to Margate and Ramsgate, by way of the Midland, Metropolitan widened lines and L.C. & D.R. As the district developed additional stations were opened in the Tottenham area, first at Harringay Park (Green Lanes) in 1880 and at St. Ann's Road (at the junction of Seven Sisters Road) in October, 1882. The latter was closed to all traffic on 9th August, 1942.

In connection with the opening of St. Ann's Road station there is an interesting notice to be found in the *Tottenham and Edmonton Weekly Herald* for Friday, 6th October, 1882, which is worth reproducing as an example of the kind of thing that occurred in Victorian times when a new railway or station was opened. Here is the extract : " On Monday morning last the new station on the Tottenham and Hampstead Junction Railway erected for the accommodation of the large and increasing districts of St. Ann's was opened for public traffic. Originally it was intended that the opening should take place on 1st June last, but unavoidable delays prevented the arrangement being carried out. All the trains from Sth. Tottenham to Moorgate St. will now stop at the new station, which will be a boon to the neighbourhood as hitherto travellers from St. Ann's Road had to go either to Stamford Hill or Seven Sisters stations on the G.E. system. The opening was regarded with great satisfaction in the locality, flags of all nations supplied by Messrs. Eveniss and Pike, proprietors of the Victoria Tavern, St. Ann's Road, were suspended from one side of the road to the other, and various tradesmen met to congratulate themselves upon the long deferred benefit having come at last. There is no doubt whatever that the new station will largely add to the prosperity of St. Ann's district, by bringing to it a considerable number of additional residents, the want of proper railway accommodation having hitherto been a great drawback. On Monday evening there was a brilliant display of fireworks from an elevated position of the Victoria Tavern. A large crowd assembled, but everything passed off without a hitch of any kind.''

How different was the closing, not a protest, or even a sigh of regret. The booking office doors just closed for the last time and next day a disinterested public passed by quite oblivious of the fact that almost exactly sixty years earlier those same doors had opened to the accompaniment of fireworks.

A Bill to provide for the transfer of the T. & H.R. to the Midland and Great Eastern companies was thrown out on 24th March, 1871, but eventually on 1st July, 1902, the transfer took place under a joint committee, the title being changed to the Tottenham and Hampstead Joint Committee, and the arrangement exists to this day.

The traffic on the T. & H.R. has always been fairly intensive and the pair of tracks are always fully employed. On 26th July, 1901, an Act was passed empowering the company to widen their property to allow additional tracks to be laid down. The powers obtained were never exercised and they expired on 26th July, 1904. The Act contains some interesting details concerning the sizes of the various bridges spanning roadways and other railways.

Now must follow the story of the development of an important link in London's outer suburban railway system, and one which was of great benefit to Tottenham residents as its completion gave a direct route to the City. It was obvious that this route as an alternative to the one via Stratford was badly needed by Tottenham and Edmonton. With this in view the Great Eastern applied for powers to construct their line from Bethnal Green to Edmonton to link up with the already existing branch line from Angel Road, Edmonton, to Enfield Town. At the same time the company sought powers to construct their great metropolitan terminus at Liverpool Street as the Bishopsgate (known as Shoreditch) terminus was fast becoming too small for the traffic it was being called upon to handle. The new railway had also the additional advantage of passing right through the centre of Tottenham, which offset the inconvenience of the one-sided situation of the Northumberland Park and Tottenham stations.

In 1864, the Great Eastern obtained the Royal Assent to these Bills, and in the local press of the time the project was hailed with much delight and the local populace had visions of a speedy train service to Town, but any hopes of these prospects being quickly matured were soon doomed to disappointment as it was not until the 22nd July, 1872, that the first train entered the district over the new line.

Actually a scheme for a direct line from the centre of Tottenham to the City was first heard about in 1863, when the *Tottenham and Edmonton Advertiser* for 1st July, 1863, stated that the Great Eastern intended to construct a railway from Broad Street through Dalston, Stoke Newington, Tottenham and so to Enfield, and that this would entail passing through some 367 houses, gardens and pastures in Tottenham alone.

After the passing of the Act in 1864, things began to move and notices were soon served upon about 500 property owners in Tottenham through which the proposed line would run. In the October of 1864, the actual notices of survey were served and a note of interest to local residents appeared in the *Tottenham and Edmonton Advertiser* for that month which gave the following information : " We believe the Company intend to erect a station a little to the southward of Bruce Grove ; this will cause the removal of the Ship Inn and several houses in its immediate neighbourhood, which will be no slight addition to the improvements now going on in that part of the High Road." It is rather unusual to find a newspaper, even for those times, suggesting that a new railway would be the means of actually improving the local amenities.

By March, 1865, it was reported that negotiations with the land-owners were proceeding satisfactorily, and by the following November the local press was optimistic enough to prophesy that a half-hourly train service would be introduced, but they little thought that nearly seven years were to elapse before the trains started to run at all, and it was not until October, 1869, that any suggestion was made of the construction work being commenced, when tenders were put out for the construction in one mile lengths. By the May of 1870, work was really in hand and Tottenham residents could at last see things taking shape.

In the August of 1869, a public meeting was held in the local Lecture Hall to demand the introduction of workmen's fares on the new line when it should eventually be opened. The *Tottenham and Edmonton Advertiser*, evidently favouring that section of its readers known as the " upper classes," did not take kindly to this meeting and a rather remarkable report was published concerning it. The paper was sorry to hear that the new line might run workmen's trains, as in their opinion there did not appear to be any demand for them, and they would only encourage a large body of people who could not fail to add to poverty and mortality and an increase in the local rates. The report also asked if it was fair to ask the proprietors of the railway to use their property at a loss and pointed out that the North London Railway's early morning trains carried only about 240 people daily, for which they paid in fares a total sum of one pound only. The meeting apparently failed in its object at which the paper expressed no regrets. As a point of interest, early morning workmen's tickets were issued by certain trains between Enfield Town and Liverpool Street (and intermediate stations) for many years at the extraordinary low fare of 2d. return. These 2d. fares were probably amongst the cheapest in the country.

One or two points of interest can be recorded concerning the construction of the railway. It was originally intended that the right angle crossing with the T. & H.R. should be on the same level, but evidently the two companies thought better of this proposal as it must have been apparent even in those days that a dead-level crossing of two such suburban lines would be a great hindrance to train working. The Great Eastern, therefore, obtained an additional Act in 1866 which allowed them to raise the level of their railway so as to provide a distance of 16 ft. 9 in. between rail levels. A sectional drawing of this length of the railway is reproduced on page 30, and this was taken from a copy of the deposited plans in respect of this alteration. Where these two railways cross each other there is still a large tract of open land which has resulted from the original undeveloped schemes to connect the two lines by means of three triangular junctions, as will be seen from the accompanying plan. Curiously enough, however, none of these three connections came to maturity, excepting railway No. 5, in the south-east corner, which was partly erected and the embankment raised to rail level ; it still remains to this day in this unfinished state and, with the remainder of the land, is used for railway allotments. A link was eventually built between the two lines, but in the north-east corner, thus giving direct communication between Seven Sisters and South Tottenham stations. This was opened on 1st June, 1880, and enabled the through trains from Palace Gates to Stratford, and later in 1887 to Woolwich, to operate.

The matter of these connecting lines was again raised later, for the Great Eastern Railway (General Powers) Act, passed on 25th July, 1890, empowered the company to build a connecting link in the north-western corner of the junctions. This was to be 1 furlong, $3\frac{1}{2}$ chains in length and to commence from the T. & H.R. some 9 chains west of the bridge carrying the Enfield line and connecting with the latter about $7\frac{1}{2}$ chains north from the T. & H.R. This link was never constructed, which, perhaps, was unfortunate as it would have enabled a through service to be operated between Enfield or Edmonton and St. Pancras.

The next development in Tottenham's railway system was the promotion and construction of the branch line from Seven Sisters Junction to Palace Gates (Wood

Green). The Bill authorising this line was passed on 16th July, 1874. The railway is 2 miles 5 furlongs in length and at Palace Gates the company laid out a large storage yard for rolling stock as well as a spacious passenger station. An earlier scheme for a line to Alexandra Park from Seven Sisters was promoted in 1866, for on Stanford's Metropolitan Railways Map for lines sanctioned in 1866 the proposed railway is shown following the route as existing to-day as far as Palace Gates station, and then continuing on by means of a huge semi-circular loop through New Southgate and Colney Hatch to link up with the diminutive Muswell Hill Railway, which short line was promoted to link Muswell Hill itself with the Palace building, a distance of approximately half a mile. The 1874 Act did not provide for the line to run beyond Palace Gates.

After the grouping in 1923 the L.N.E.R. laid in a connecting line between the Palace Gates yard and Bowes Park station on the Enfield and Hertford branch of the late Great Northern. This at first was only a single line connection, but in 1944 it was made into a normal double junction. This is a very valuable link between the Great Eastern and Great Northern sections and has been of good use on several occasions, as will be told in the train working chapter.

Traffic commenced to operate on the Palace Gates branch on 1st January, 1878, but only between Seven Sisters and Green Lanes (now called Noel Park and Wood Green), the remaining section being opened on 7th October following. A station was opened at West Green at the junction of West Green Road and Philip Lane, and this encouraged the development of this small village which at that time was quite distinct from the main part of Tottenham.

The story now comes to the final phase of the railways as they exist to-day. This was the construction of the Forest Gate line. This railway was called the Tottenham and Forest Gate Railway and the Act of Parliament authorising its construction was passed on 4th August, 1890, and it was opened to traffic on 9th July, 1894. It was jointly promoted by the Midland and London, Tilbury and Southend companies and it connected the T. & H.R. at South Tottenham with Woodgrange Park, thus providing a through line from St. Pancras to Tilbury and Southend-on-Sea. This was a very valuable link for the Midland, especially as they purchased the London, Tilbury and Southend undertaking in 1912, and so became sole proprietors of the Forest Gate line. The opening of this railway was of considerable benefit to Tottenham residents as it afforded them direct communication with Walthamstow, Leyton, Ilford, Barking and other places in South Essex, which heretofore could only be approached by roundabout journeys. The through trains to Southend-on-Sea were of great value, as they gave local people the opportunity to spend a day or longer beside the sea at a low cost in fares. What was more important to the Midland was the fact that they were able to run through expresses to Tilbury in connection with ocean-going liners.

The construction of the original T. & H.R. was of considerable importance in itself, but its value as a connecting link was greatly increased by the opening of the Forest Gate line, and it can now be rightly regarded as the main connection between the Thames Estuary and all the trunk lines entering London on the west and north-west.

A   Description
of the Railways

CHAPTER II

GENERAL

THE railways within the Tottenham area are not without some interesting engineering features, a brief description of which now follows. The main line retains still a certain atmosphere inherited from early Great Eastern times, and passing as it does along the floor of the Lea Valley, the gradients are naturally easy, that between the Hale and Northumberland Park stations being only 1 in 1,071, rising towards the latter. There are four running roads, the slow being on the east side, and laid down in 1913 in order to relieve the pressure on the fast roads. These slow roads extend down as far as Pickett's Lock, just north of Edmonton, and an interesting feature regarding them, apart from the signalling which will be explained later, is that they have no physical connection with the north or south junction ; a double cross-over is provided at Northumberland Park for the exchange of traffic between the slow and fast lines.

The north and south junctions are situated between the bridge over the River Lea and Tottenham station ; the latter junction has the switches almost on the bridge itself, and the curve leading away to the T. & H.R. at the West Junction is an extremely sharp one, having a radius of only 7 chains, but the other leg of the triangle is much less severe.

From its junction with the L.N.E.R. at the North Junction, the T. & H.R. gradually climbs to South Tottenham station whence it is carried on an embankment right across the Borough. After leaving South Tottenham station there is a slight drop at 1 in 100 to pass under the L.N.E.R. Hackney Downs—Enfield line, after which the line climbs all the way to beyond Crouch Hill, slightly at first but afterwards as steeply as 1 in 100, which makes it hard going for west bound freight trains.

A very unusual feature of this length of railway is the provision of two sets of mile posts ; those on the north side of the line are the original ones and measure the T. & H.R., the calculations being from the North Junction to Gospel Oak ; the others are on the south side and indicate the mileage from St. Pancras to Woodgrange Park, and they were erected when the Forest Gate line was opened in 1894.

The connecting curve between South Tottenham station and Seven Sisters Junction is also on an embankment, laid on a curve on $6\frac{1}{4}$ chains radius with a rising gradient of 1 in 110 towards the latter place. This curve is a severe test to any locomotive obliged to work round it when hauling a load near its maximum capacity. This length of railway is the property of the L.N.E.R. and not the L.M.S.R. as is shown on some maps in existence.

The Forest Gate line, which is the property of the L.M.S.R., is remarkable for its great number of bridges, both over and under roadways and extensive brick viaducts ; the viaduct between Queen's Road, Leyton, goods depôt and Wanstead comprises no fewer than 386 arches, 350 of which have a span of 30 feet each. This railway enters the Tottenham district when it passes over the old River Lea, the actual boundary being on the west bank of the river, which happens also to be the Middlesex and Essex county boundary. A short embankment separates the old river from the modern Lea Navigation which is crossed by a substantial bridge, to be followed by a three-span plate girder bridge over the L.N.E.R. main line just above the North Junction ; between this bridge and South Tottenham there is a brick viaduct of some length.

The Enfield line of the L.N.E.R. enters the district in a deep cutting at Stamford Hill station, about one-third of which is within the Borough. This cutting opens out on to an embankment and continues across the open space where it crosses over the T. & H.R. earlier described. This crossing is made by means of a rather frail looking three-span bridge which has the effect of looking rather elevated, as the T. & H.R. is already on an embankment some 15 feet high. After passing through Seven Sisters Junction there is a medium depth cutting for about a quarter mile, after which it is embankment all the way to the Edmonton boundary ; this length includes a stretch of brick viaduct.

The only feature of the Palace Gates branch is the wide cutting at West Green in which is situated the station ; the gradient down from Seven Sisters to West Green is 1 in 90, after which the line rises all the way from there to Palace Gates.

STATIONS

The main Tottenham station at the Hale is a good specimen of an early Eastern Counties station. It is hopelessly out of date for modern needs, and plans and preparations were ready before the second world war for its rebuilding, but these had to be postponed upon the outbreak of hostilities ; they will, no doubt, be revived as soon as conditions allow.

The present structure is not the original one, as considerable alterations were carried out in 1859 after loud and continual complaints from a long-suffering public. There did not appear to be a footbridge connecting the two platforms and the *Tottenham and Edmonton Advertiser* was convinced that some one was certain to be killed whilst passing over the tracks to or from the up platform. One note published stated that the station (the original building) was a positive disgrace both to the district and to its owners, and it looked forward to the completion of the alterations which were to have the effect of giving Tottenham the distinction of having the best station on the line ! Apparently, the alterations involved the realignment of the railway and a new up road and platform were built behind the former up platform ; the old up road became the down line, the platform being extended out to meet it. In the coloured frontispiece, showing cattle unloading at Tottenham station in 1855, it will be noted that the down main line is next to the cattle train standing alongside the long dock. (The passenger train in the scene is an *up* one). At the present there are two tracks between the down main line and the dock platform, and this would agree with the statement that the old up road became the down line. However, the long dock is now seldom used for cattle traffic, but is, in fact, a long spare platform. The bridge carrying the Ferry Lane was lengthened to span the new lay-out.

One unusual feature of the station, and one which still exists, is the spacious " green " which fronts it, and for many years a notice informed the public that all stray cattle found upon it would be impounded ; this has long since been removed, probably because it was thought that the chance of stray cattle in present-day Tottenham is somewhat remote. The down platform, which abuts on to this green, and is level with it, contains all the offices of the station, including the station-master's house which has its front door on the platform. At the top end of the station, one wall of the large goods shed forms the back of the platform, and built into this is an unusual drinking fountain which bears the head of Queen Victoria and the date 1860. This fountain does not appear to have been erected to mark any special occasion and has nothing to do with the Queen's visit to Cambridge as described in the next chapter. Also, the illustration accompanying that description shows an elaborate canopy which had been erected for the occasion. If the drawing is correct then the small canopy which served to help keep the elements out of the booking-hall for many years was obviously erected afterwards ; however, a severe gale early in 1943 removed this structure and a smaller one still was erected some months later. On the other hand the drawing may suffer from a certain amount of artist's licence and it is possible that he exaggerated the size of the canopy to make the thing look more impressive.

The up platform, which is very low and rather dangerous to aged or infirm passengers, has a long, low open shelter only and is connected to the down side by a substantial iron footbridge.

Ferry Lane, Tottenham, is one of the few highways running across the Lea Valley and for many years was a bottle-neck between Tottenham and Walthamstow and surrounding districts. The electric trams from the latter place terminated at the Ferry Boat Inn and passengers had to walk from there into Tottenham. The road bridge at the station was strengthened a few years ago and, with the coming of the trolley-buses, powers were obtained to extend them from the Ferry Boat Inn into Tottenham. This was a great advantage although for many years previously a service of petrol buses had terminated near the station which gave transport up to the High Road via Broad Lane.

Northumberland Park station was originally called Marsh Lane, and afterwards only Park. This structure would appear to be the original one, and although the platforms are long and adequate for the traffic, the buildings and offices are small and bunched up at the top end of the down platform. The buildings occupy a considerable portion of the platform width and the resulting narrow strip remaining for pedestrians and passengers is dangerous. A special wide entrance and exit is provided for the football traffic that occurs when the Tottenham Hotspur football team is playing a home match ; the amount of traffic for these matches is about 50 per cent. of that using White Hart Lane station on the Enfield line. A substantial iron footbridge, built by Boulton & Paul, of Norwich, in 1910, connects the two platforms.

An unusual feature of the " Park " Station was the barn-like structure covering the entrance to the booking-office ; this also covered the loading dock for parcels traffic. Hardly had the writer finished drafting this chapter when the engineers decided to pull down this interesting and ancient feature which had given the station a genuine old country appearance. This work was done directly after the widening of the level crossing which here carries the Marsh Lane over on to the Lea Marshes. Originally, this narrow lane only led to the marshland beyond the railway and the narrow single road crossing was adequate for traffic of the time, but the post-1918 armistice years saw a development of the land for factory and industrial purposes and much traffic has of necessity to cross the line. Frequent and long delays occurred to road traffic (a substantial footbridge is provided for pedestrians) owing to the frequency of the rail traffic. The crossing is a bone of contention to all concerned but it seems next to impossible to provide a bridge over, or a tunnel under, the railway, owing to the development of property close up to the west side of the line, quite apart from the question of drainage—a serious problem in these parts. To assist matters, the crossing was widened during the summer of 1943 to the maximum width possible, this dimension being limited by the station building on one side and the footbridge on the other. Space was so restricted that it was necessary to remove the down fast starting signal ; this was replaced by a colour light signal a little farther down the line. However, the work was worth while as the crossing can now accommodate two lines of road traffic and this enables it to be cleared much more easily.

The chief feature of Northumberland Park is the large marshalling yard on the up side of the line. This has fourteen sorting sidings and three running roads and the whole extends nearly halfway to Tottenham station. This yard runs alongside the public recreation grounds and forms a good spot for observing freight train working.

There is no station-master's house for Northumberland Park, but a private one nearby was provided for his use until the station, some year's ago, was brought under the charge of the Angel Road master ; a separate station-master was again appointed in 1942.

On the Enfield and Palace Gates lines the stations are all spacious and well built structures in yellow stock brick to typical Great Eastern designs, those at Seven Sisters, Bruce Grove and White Hart Lane being on embankments, whilst those at Stamford Hill and West Green are in cuttings, the latter being especially wide and deep. All the stations reflect the heavy passenger traffic of bygone days, but with the conversion to electric working in the years to come, they will no doubt regain their former activity. Seven Sisters has four platforms, two for the Enfield line and two for the Palace Gates branch, and is really two separate stations. The down platform of the former and the up platform of the latter lines are joined at the London end, but the other ends are a considerable distance apart, the Palace Gates branch curving away sharply. These two platforms are also connected by a high footbridge at platform level, as well as by the subway at ground level which links all four platforms. A long footpath running parallel with the down Enfield line platform leads from this subway to the main booking office, the entrance to which fronts on to the West Green road at the northern end of Enfield line platforms ; there is a secondary booking-office (now used for early morning workmen's traffic only), situated on the far side of the Palace Gates lines and leading off the subway. When this is open it saves a considerable walk for people living on the western side of the station.

Bruce Grove and White Hart Lane stations are similar in nearly every respect to the Enfield portion of Seven Sisters, excepting that at White Hart Lane there are provided some special wide exit doors to handle the football traffic when the occasion arises. Stamford Hill and West Green stations are similar in design to the stations just mentioned, but built in reverse so to speak, by virtue of their being in cuttings. All these structures are substantial and have weathered their seventy odd years very well ; all are equipped with ample offices for the traffic and all were opened on the same day as the opening of the railways concerned. Good detached station-master's houses are provided at Seven Sisters and White Hart Lane.

On the T. & H.R. line all three stations, South Tottenham, St. Ann's Road, Harringay Park, are built to similar designs, excepting that the first named has some brick buildings on the down platform ; all are on embankments. The platforms are of wooden construction and all three stations have one feature in common and that is that the booking offices are separate, brick built, and are situated at the foot of the embankments right on the pavement level. After passing through the booking halls, the platforms are gained by means of open footpaths and stairways, with a connecting subway under the line. These three stations were not opened at the time of the opening of the railway as has been mentioned in chapter I.

GOODS YARDS

The goods yards are four in number and are well situated to serve conveniently the needs of the Borough. Harringay Park has a coal and general yard, but practically all of it is within the Hornsey Borough, although it serves chiefly the south-western corner of Tottenham Borough which embraces a greater portion of Harringay. This latter yard, as well as that at South Tottenham, is the sole property of the L.M.S.R., having been inherited from the Midland who laid out the yards at their own expense ; they are managed by a separate staff from that of the passenger stations.

The South Tottenham yard is of exceptional length, being over 1,500 feet ; it is really two separate yards connected together by a narrow neck through which runs one track that divides into two long sidings. This yard deals mostly in coal, but has some general traffic.

The three L.N.E.R. yards are situated at the Hale, White Hart Lane and West Green, and all have good siding accommodation and are provided with all necessary cranes, banks and weigh-bridges, etc. ; at Tottenham station (the Hale) there is a lofty goods shed of typical Great Eastern design.

All kinds of merchandise and minerals are dealt with at Tottenham main yard, but at White Hart Lane and West Green the traffic is mainly coal and builders' merchants' materials.

PRIVATE SIDINGS

There are a number of private sidings in the district and these are shown on the detailed map. Leading off the Tottenham goods yard shunting neck is a siding running into the Corporation dust destructor works ; in the work's yard there is a modern ash loading plant. Beyond Northumberland Park and leading off the down main line in the *facing* direction is a siding serving other sidings leading into the main works of the Tottenham and District Gas Company's works. On the Enfield line, just north of Seven Sisters station, one siding leads off into some short spurs serving several buildings and there is also a siding into the Town Hall yard which the Corporation uses as a general storage ground. This latter siding has two roads, complete with platforms and shunting capstans. These sidings are shown on the R.C.H. Junction diagrams in the latter part of the nineteenth century as Seven Sisters Goods.

BRIDGES

First amongst these are the two parallel spans carrying the main line over the Lea Navigation. They are of simple plate girder construction, each with a skew span of 84 ft. 6 in. ; they are very close to the water, the headway for river craft being only 10 feet.

The bridge carrying the L.M.S.R. Forest Gate line over the L.N.E.R. main line has three spans of plate girder construction, supported on brick piers. To carry this line across the River Lea there are two spans of plate girder construction, one span crossing the water, and the other the wide bank on the east side. This additional span was probably put in to allow for the free flow of the flood water that used to be very prevalent in winter time until a few years ago. A plate girder span carries the line over the Lea Navigation. Between the L.N.E.R. main line and the junction at South Tottenham there is a substantial brick viaduct consisting of twenty-four arches and one span, on the skew, of plate girder construction. The total length of this viaduct is about 900 feet, which together with the other bridges just described makes a total length of bridgework between the South Tottenham Junction and the Tottenham boundary of approximately 1,400 feet in a distance of about 3,900 feet.

The bridge carrying the L.N.E.R. Enfield line over the T. & H. R. line is a frail looking affair of three short spans of open wooden deck supported on under girders and brick piers. Between Bruce Grove and White Hart Lane stations there is another length of brick viaduct comprising twenty-one arches, which has a total length of just over 600 feet, including three plate girder bridges over side roads. There are a further eight plate girder bridges over side roads between White Hart Lane and Seven Sisters and all these were overhauled and strengthened between 1942 and 1944.

The bridge carrying the T. & H.R. line over the junction of the Seven Sisters and St. Ann's roads, is a massive affair, and is unusual in that the up side has one span and the down side two spans, the latter being supported in the centre by a massive

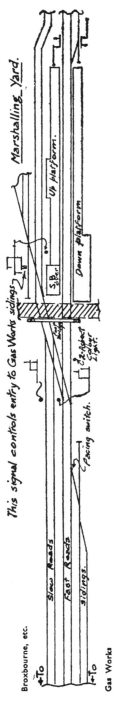

This signal controls entry to Gas Works sidings

Marshalling Yard.

Broxbourne, etc.

Slow Roads

Fast Roads

sidings.

Gas Works

The layout at Northumberland Park station on the main line showing the unusual arrangement of sidings leading off the down fast road in the facing direction. The shaded portion indicates the position of the level crossing.

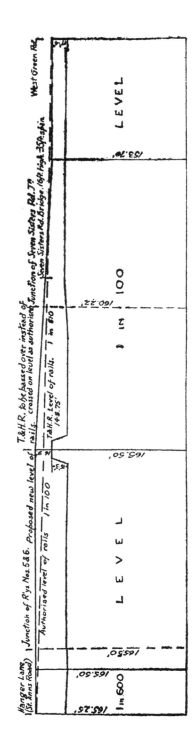

An extract from the deposited plans of the G.E.R. (Additional Powers) Act, 1866 showing the deviation of levels of Railway No. 3 of G.E.R. Metropolitan Station and Railways Act, 1864 as originally proposed to be constructed.

The datum line was 138·27 feet below the upper surface of the stone in the centre of the western gate of Grove Villas in the West Green Road, Tottenham, being 100 feet below published Ordnance datum.

brick pier, some six or seven feet square, which stands in the middle of the roadways.

There are several other minor road bridges in the district, all of various designs and construction, and also some all metal foot-bridges.

SIGNALLING

On the main line the signalling is mechanical with Sykes' lock-and-block apparatus. The signals are all semaphore, excepting the down fast starting signals at Tottenham and Northumberland Park stations, which are colour-lights mechanically controlled. For the fast roads and the North and South Junctions, the lay-out of the signalling is in the orthodox manner and calls for no special comment. The slow roads, however, are worked on the permissive sight principle and the semaphore arms are about half normal size, some being of the open scissor type. As there is no block working on these slow roads, the signals are only situated where there is some obstruction, such as a level crossing, or where some other road fouls the running lines. These signals are normally kept in the *off* position and are only placed to the *on* position when it is necessary to obstruct the running by crossing gates or other trains fouling the slow roads by passing across from sidings to the fast roads ; the signals only indicate the state of the road at the point of their situation, but do not indicate if the line ahead is occupied or not. At Northumberland Park, on the down slow road, there is a three-arm bracket signal, one arm of which is of standard size and this controls the starting of trains from the slow road over on to the fast road ; the right-hand little arm governs the straight run through on the slow road, whilst the left-hand small arm has the very unusual function of governing the entry into a *facing* siding on the *fast down* road some one hundred yards or so beyond the station (see diagram).

The Northumberland Park signal box is of unusual design, being high above the ground supported on four posts, spanning the approach to the up platform, and commands a fine view of the surrounding railway. By contrast, Tottenham station box is tucked between the road-bridge and the platform, and the signalman has to lean out of a window to view most train movements.

The Enfield line has automatic colour-light signalling installed during 1934 by the Westinghouse Brake and Signal Company. These signals are of the three- and four-aspect searchlight type, controlled by a.c. track circuits, with the exception of Seven Sisters Junction. At the latter box there are no automatic colour-light signals, but the up Enfield line starting signals for the junction to South Tottenham are colour-lights controlled by levers in the box. The junction is mechanically controlled owing to this system still being in use on the Palace Gates line and the curve down to South Tottenham. The signal-box has three illuminated diagrams : (*a*) the Hackney Downs—Seven Sisters diagram with the down line circuits indicated by lights ; (*b*) the Seven

Sisters—Edmonton diagram with the up line illuminated when unoccupied ; (c) the Seven Sisters Junction territory diagram with both lines indicated by lights. There is a ground frame at Seven Sisters that controls the entrance into the Town Hall siding group, and also two frames at White Hart Lane for the goods yard ; the latter are under the joint control of the Seven Sisters Junction and Edmonton Junction boxes.

The T. & H.R. has mechanical signalling with Midland single needle block telegraph, excepting between the West and North Junctions, which is Tyer's block telegraph. At South Tottenham there is the feature of the distant arms for the next sections on the T. & H.R. being placed under the respective starting signals, although there are advanced starting signals farther out, but at the time of writing, however, there are signs that new upper quadrant advance starters are being erected in which case repeating distant arms will be placed on the same post. Also, with the closing of St. Anns Road station, there is the suggestion that the signal box be closed and an automatic block section be substituted, which would be quite sufficient for operational purposes.

The signalling within the district is quite interesting and there are various types of block telegraphs in use, and to make a permanent record of these, with details of the signal boxes, the writer has prepared a table which will be found at the end of this book as Appendix B.

CHAPTER III   Incidents and Accidents

ONE of the earliest incidents in the history of the Tottenham railways, and probably one of the most important, was the visit of Queen Victoria and the Prince Consort in 1847. It was on the occasion of their journey and visit to Cambridge when His Royal Highness was installed as Prince Chancellor of the University. This was on the 5th July, 1847, and not only was the journey of interest to the local inhabitants, but it was also one of great importance to Mr. George Hudson, then Chairman of the Eastern Counties Railway as was mentioned in the first chapter. Always ready to seize upon any opportunity for publicity, the famous Railway King did not fail to live up to his reputation upon this occasion ; it was too great a chance to let slip by, for at that time the fortunes of the Eastern

Counties were at a very low ebb, and the fact that Queen Victoria had chosen to travel over its lines naturally brought the whole thing into the public eye—publicity of the first order.

The Royal Party drove from Buckingham Palace to Tottenham station where Mr. Hudson and Mr. Waddington, together with other directors and officers of the railway company, were waiting to receive them. The station was altered to provide a Royal reception room, and a special canopy was erected at the entrance. The Royal train consisted of the special Royal saloon which the Eastern Counties had borrowed from the L. & N.W.R., three first-class carriages, and two brake-vans ; the train was preceded by a pilot engine, as became the custom for all Royal trains for many years afterwards, to ensure a safe passage for the train. After the usual introductions and presentations and mutual congratulations the train started on its journey for Cambridge at 11.20 a.m., and arrived at its destination at 1.8 p.m.

An early drawing depicting the arrival of Queen Victoria at Tottenham station for her journey to Cambridge, showing the specially constructed pavilion.

The return journey was made on the following Wednesday afternoon, and the arrival time at Tottenham was at 4.23 p.m., and as on the outward journey, Messrs. Hudson and Waddington accompanied the Royal Party, and on arrival at Tottenham Her Majesty expressed herself as being very pleased with all the arrangements for the journeys, the Prince Consort personally conveying the message to Hudson, who, no doubt, was highly gratified at the fact that everything had gone off without mishap.

There is a popular local belief that the Queen started her rail journey from Tottenham because it was the terminus of the line. This, of course, is not so as from the commencement the railway had operated from Stratford and afterwards from Shoreditch. The probable reason for the decision was that the drive to Tottenham was considered more attractive than it would have been to Shoreditch, and also eight miles of rail journey (through a very poor locality for the first part) was saved. Another reason, although it is only the writer's suggestion, may be that the large green fronting Tottenham Station might have been considered more suitable for the reception of the Royal Party as allowing a greater number of people to see it.

Although the event just described is the only occasion on which Royalty have actually commenced and finished a journey from a Tottenham station, it is certainly by no means the only time that Royalty and other distinguished visitors have passed through the district. Indeed, it is probable that the Tottenham and Hampstead Joint line has seen the passage of more Royal specials than any other line in the Kingdom.

The earliest record of a Royal special after the formation of the Great Eastern, was on the occasion of the marriage of King Edward VII and Queen Alexandra (then the Prince and Princess of Wales) on 10th March, 1863. This train was worked from London (Shoreditch) to King's Lynn by the Sinclair single-driver express, engine No. 284, which was driven by Alexander Kerr ; to mark the occasion the locomotive was painted cream and garlanded. On two other occasions Royal weddings called for special trains that passed through Tottenham. The first was that of the wedding of the Duke and Duchess of York (afterwards King George V and Queen Mary) on 6th July, 1893. This special ran from Liverpool Street, departing at 5.30 p.m. and was hauled to King's Lynn by oil-fired 2—4—0 locomotive No. 761 (Class T19). A coronet mounted on a cushion adorned the top of the smoke-box, while the Royal coat-of-arms was placed over the centre of the buffer beam. The second event was on July 22nd, 1896, for the wedding of Prince Charles of Denmark, a special train being run from St. Pancras to Wolferton (the station for Sandringham). Departure time was 5.45 p.m. and the train ran non-stop to Lynn, and again an oil-burning 2—4—0 locomotive was used, No. 712.

On 28th January, 1892, locomotive No. 755, of 2—4—0 T19 class, driven by John Wright, of Stratford, hauled the funeral special conveying the remains of the Duke of Clarence through from King's Lynn to Windsor. A two-day visit by the Emperor William II of Germany to Sandringham kept the Great Eastern and the Tottenham main line busy at the close of last century. A Royal special ran from Windsor to Wolferton on 25th November, 1899, and a corresponding return trip was made two days later, but the train ran into Liverpool Street and not to Windsor, as it was worked through to Port Victoria on the S.E. & C.R. via the East London Railway.

After the death of Queen Victoria the number of Royal journeys to Sandringham increased tremendously owing to the fact that both King Edward VII and King George V seemed to prefer their Norfolk residence to all others. Practically all these trains departed from or arrived at St. Pancras when the Royal party were not at Windsor, and in the latter case the special trains worked right through from Windsor to Sandringham via the Tottenham and Hampstead joint line. All these Royal specials were worked throughout their journeys by Great Eastern locomotives, including the run over the Midland and Great Western Railways. The chief reasons why Liverpool Street station was rarely used for such Royal specials was partly owing to the congestion of traffic on both road and rail at that end of the City, and also to avoid constant repetition of certain formalities which had to be enacted whenever His Majesty the King came within the City of London boundary, such as the presentation of the Sword of the City by the Lord Mayor of London.

Other Royal specials to pass through Tottenham in Great Eastern days included those conveying the Royal Family through from King's Lynn to Windsor for the christening ceremony of Prince John in August, 1905 ; the Emperor William II of Germany again on 8th November, 1902 ; the King of Norway on 25th November, 1908 ; Her Imperial Majesty the Empress of Russia on 16th August, 1910 ; the King of Denmark on 16th August, 1913.

It would probably only be tedious to the reader to give a complete list of all the Royal specials and other trains conveying Royalty which have passed through Tottenham, but it can be seen that the Tottenham main line justifies the title of the " Royal Route." In recent years following the grouping, Royal trains now work into and from King's Cross running via Hitchin and Royston, but Tottenham has not lost all touch with trains conveying Royalty as, in peace-time, special trains are run from Tilbury to St. Pancras, and vice versa, in connection with ocean-going liners, and visiting Royalty frequently use this route.

Tottenham evidently had some attraction for holiday makers in early Victorian times, for a note is to be found in the *Tottenham and Edmonton Advertiser* dated 1st July, 1870, to the effect that 15,000 visitors arrived at the Hale Station on the previous Whit Monday. This necessitated the use of twenty-eight special trains, and in the eyes of the local paper this was a remarkable feat in view of the fact that no mishap occurred. This huge excursion traffic is certainly non-existent to-day, although large numbers of people invade the Borough on certain Saturdays in the winter months, but they come for quite a different purpose than that of holiday making ; they are the supporters of the famous Tottenham Hotspur Football Club, whose ground is situated near the White Hart Lane station on the Enfield line, and about a half-mile from the Northumberland Park station on the main line.

For many years before private motoring became so cheap and popular, the two stations handled an enormous passenger traffic in respect of these football excursions, but in recent years it has naturally tended to fall off, but even so it is still considerable as will be seen by the figures for the last season before the outbreak of war in September, 1939 ; they are as follows : Total arrivals at White Hart Lane, 163,640 passengers with an average of 4,034 ; the highest number on any one day being 10,300 and the lowest 90, so the reader can judge for himself the difficulty of providing for so fluctuating a traffic. The railway has the advantage, however, of not cluttering up the public roads with thousands of small cars, coaches and 'buses, as happens when a large number of people descend by road upon one place at one and the same time.

In the so-called golden days of pre-1914 the football traffic was at its height and anyone travelling over a mile or so used the train, and it may not be out of place to give a brief indication of the method employed at White Hart Lane to cope with the enormous pressure of so dense a passenger traffic. As mentioned in chapter two, the station is provided with special exit doors, and on the football days the station-master and his staff were supplemented by additional inspectors, ticket-collectors and police. Little trouble was experienced in clearing the station as each train came in following one another as closely as train working would allow. The empties were worked down to Enfield for storage and marshalling ready for the return journeys. special excursion trains were worked in between the ordinary trains in the time-table. Getting the crowds away again after the match was a sterner job for the officials, and much depended upon the result of the game as to the mood of the " followers." As the crowd descended upon the station they were marshalled into orderly queues by mounted policemen. In the meantime the first train had been worked up from Enfield to await in a nearby siding, and as the time-table allowed, this and the following ordinary and " specials," were brought into the station to pick up the crowds who were allowed up on to the platform in sufficient numbers to fill each train ; departures were at intervals of five minutes or less. A crowd of seven to eight thousand used to be cleared in just over the half-hour, and it is interesting to note that nearly one hundred ordinary 'buses would be required to shift the same number of people. White Hart Lane in those days certainly demonstrated the ability of the railway as a means of transport to move large numbers of people quickly, cheaply and in safety and without undue inconvenience and congestion to people using the local highways.

The traffic at Northumberland Park was never so heavy as at the "Lane," and the writer is informed by the company that it was approximately 50 per cent. of the latter's total.

Several serious railway accidents have taken place within the Tottenham district, and they are all concerned with the main line. One of the earliest, although it cannot actually be classed as serious, is interesting if only for the remarks concerning it which appeared in the local press at the time. It was on the 12th September, 1858, that an excursion train collided with some empty wagons just north of the Hale station. About twenty wagons had been shunted on to the main line and what happened can best be described by repeating the words as printed in the local paper : ". . . by some accident the more distant semaphore, which should have warned the approaching train of an obstruction on the line, was not made use of. The engine driver, on perceiving the wagons in his way, appears to have done his utmost to stop his train, and to have succeeded in reducing the speed of the train to some four or five miles per hour before the collision took place ; credit is also due to the guard for the exertions he made. Though some bruises were sustained, no passengers were seriously hurt, and all but one went on to Rye House. We understand however that many claims have since been preferred against the Company for alleged injuries ! A brake-van, attached to the wagons, was a good deal knocked about, but no further damage appears to have been done. We understand that arrangements are being made for the regulating of trains on this line by a telegraphic system, somewhat similar we presume to that in vogue on the London and North Western Railway ; a system that will effectually prevent collisions such as the one described."

The last lines now read rather strangely and their author was an optimist, to say the least.

A far more serious affair occured, also at the Hale Station about eighteen months later, and on this occasion seven persons lost their lives ; they were the driver, fireman, and five passengers. The date of this disaster was the 20th February, 1860, and it was caused by a defective tyre on one of the leading wheels of the engine hauling the train, which was the 7.30 a.m. from Cambridge ; it was made up consisting of the locomotive (No. 103), tender, guard's-van, eight carriages and a horse-box. By a rather remarkable coincidence, Mr. Robert Sinclair, then Locomotive Superintendent to the Eastern Counties Railway, chanced to be standing on the station at the time of the accident. (He had been the Locomotive Superintendent for about two and a half years). Later in the day he wrote a long letter to the Directors which is reprinted here in full :

E.C.R. Engineer's Office,
Stratford.
20th February, 1860.

To the Directors of the Eastern Counties Railway Company.

Gentlemen,

As I happened to be an eye-witness of the lamentable accident which occurred this morning at Tottenham Station, I think it right to inform you briefly what fell under my observation.

I was in the waiting-room of the station, having just had a few words of conversation with the station-master about the Enfield up train, and was coming on the platform on hearing a train approach, when I heard an exclamation from the station people, and on looking towards the approaching train, which I should think was running at about its usual speed, I distinctly observed a bright-sided carriage rolling towards the up-side of the line. I noticed also that the engine was off the line towards the up-side. On reaching the platform the engine struck it and turned completely over, the tender flying completely over it. The carriage or van next to the tender was thrown against the engine and I saw the roof of it broken off. The next carriage was thrown against the platform wall on the up-side; the next carriage was off the rails. I should mention that, in turning over, the water and steam were discharged from the boiler, and a cloud of steam enveloped the debris as soon as I noticed what I have described.

On running along the platform I saw and heard the station-master giving orders to one of his men to put on both the up and down signals to stop trains in both directions, and this I think it right to mention in justice to the station-master, because some gentleman mentioned to me that he did not think this had been done.

What I have described occurred almost momentarily, and before I reached the site of the accident. For some little time I was unable to render personal assistance, but I went to each carriage and saw by the kind exertions of the uninjured passengers and the assistance of the station people, the wounded passengers were being got out. I saw seven persons in all, helpless and apparently seriously hurt ; the unfortunate fireman, evidently dead, lying under the engine. On looking about for the cause of the accident I observed that the tyre of one of the leading wheels was off the wheel, broken in several places, and appearances which indicated a flaw of some extent. The quality of the iron where it had severed appeared to be of the best description, and when further enquiry is made I have no doubt it will be found to be of the best Yorkshire iron. Until the result of the complete investigation I am able to give you no more information,

All photographs by
the Author unless
otherwise indicated

THE RAILWAYS OF TOTTENHAM
PICTORIAL
SECTION

A heavy metal drinking fountain built into the wall of the goods shed which
flanks the back of the down platform of Tottenham station. It carries the
crowned head of Queen Victoria and the date 1860. A few feet to the left stands
the sixth mile-post from Liverpool Street (via Clapton).

NORTHUMBERLAND PARK STATION

(Above) *An up train passing the southern end of the marshalling yards.*

(Below) *A view of the station looking north showing the unusual type of signal box. The footbridge in the foreground was erected in 1910.* (Official L.N.E.R. photograph.)

(Above) *A view of the station looking south. The building by footbridge is the station-master's house, the front door of ch is on the platform.*

(Below) *The exterior of the station showing part of the large reen". The photograph was taken in 1945.*

TOTTENHAM STATION

A general view of the wreck. ACCIDENT TO LIVERPOOL STREET—NORWICH EXPRES

The bridge in the background carries the L.M.S.R. line from South Tottenham to Woodgrange Park

TOTTENHAM NORTH JUNCTION ON 29th OCTOBER, 1929   *Raising the tender*

In the background can be seen a down passenger train working over the slow line as an emergency measure

The locomotive poised
ready for re-railing.

The locomotive is 4—6—0 No. 2808
Gunton, of the " Sandringham "
class

A close view of the wrecked locomotive showing a wagon completely smashed.

The photographs on this and the three preceding pages by courtesy of Messrs. J. Dickinson & Son, Ltd.

(Above) A N. Woolwich—Palace Gates train composed of ex-G.E. stock and 2—4—2 locomotive of L.N.E.R. Class F.5 coming up the 1—110, $6\frac{1}{4}$ chains curve between South Tottenham Junction and Seven Sisters Junction.

(Below) The Palace Gates branch at West Green, the station being just visible beyond the third arch. The view is interesting as showing a good example of the G.E.R practice of placing signals well away from the track where thought necessary.

(Above) The T. & H.R. looking west. The closed St. Ann's Road station can be seen in the distance behind the two signals. The large building in the far distance is the Harringay Arena. On the left can be seen the partly constructed embankment mentioned on page 21.

(Below) A view of the main line photographed from the L.M.S.R. bridge showing Tottenham station in distance. The Basildon works of Messrs. J. Dickinson & Son, Ltd. are on the left. The long cattle dock seen in the colour frontispiece is clearly shown here on the left.

SEVEN SISTERS JUNCTION

(Above) *A view looking south showing a Liverpool Street–Enfield train approaching from Stamford Hill. The 10 m.p.h. speed limit is for trains descending to Sth Tottenham Jnc.*

fifty

(Below) *The twin stations showing Enfield line on right and Palace Gates line on left.*

(Above) *The main line looking towards the South Junction and London. The line in the right-hand corner is the commencement of the T. & H.R.*
(Below) *Tottenham signal-box tucked away in an angle of the bridge and station.*

(Above) The main line looking north showing the principal works of the Tottenham and District Gas Company on left. The bridge is the boundary of Tottenham and Edmonton.

(Below) Another view of the main line between the North Junction and Tottenham station. The trains are being washed and cleaned out prior to returning to Liverpool Street.

SOUTH TOTTENHAM JUNCTION

(Above) *A view of the station (looking east), the full title of which is South Tottenham and Stamford Hill.*

(Below) *The junction of the Forest Gate line with the T. & H.R. The former actually starts at the home signal —seen in the left middle distance.*

fifty-three

(Right) A typical G.E.R. pattern bracket signal still in use at Northumberland Park.

(Lower right) A through Liverpool Street—Palace Gates train leaving Seven Sisters Junction for West Green. This view shows one of the very long trains of four-wheelers hauled by the little 0—6—0 "Jubilee" tank locomotives (that seen is L.N.E.R. No. 7087). Photograph taken by K. A. C. R. Nunn, in 1925, after grouping.

(Lower left) The original down home signal on the T. & H.R. at South Tottenham being replaced by upper quadrants in 1942. Official L.N.E.R. photograph.

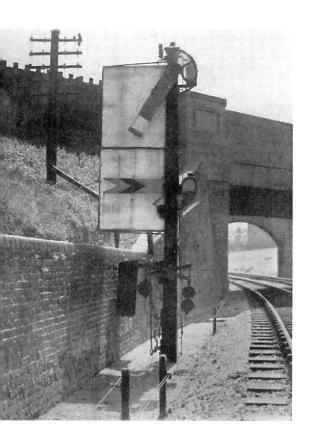

(Left) *The advance starting signal at West Green, with the Seven Sisters Junction distant, of distinctly Great Eastern vintage.*

(Lower left) *The 0—6—0 " Jubilee " tank locomotive No. 1265 damaged at Northumberland Park in January, 1931 (see page 66) awaiting scrap at Stratford. Photograph by K. A. C. R. Nunn.*

(Lower right) *A typical G.E.R. pattern home signal in use on the T. & H.R. This one, the home signal on the curve at South Tottenham from Seven Sisters Junction, was replaced in 1942 by a new upper quadrant on steel post. Official L.N.E.R. photograph.*

Local freight train on its way from Manor Road Sidings (Stoke Newington) to White Hart Lane, here seen passing Seven Sisters Junction hauled by an U.S.A. 2—8—0 locomotive.

TWO FAMOUS LOCOMOTIVES

The 4—4—0 Midland Railway No. 1757, named Beatrice, *here seen at Kentish Town on 16th April, 1902, and the G.E.R. 2—4—0 No. 760, named* Petrolea. *(Photographs by courtesy of K. A. C. R. Nunn.)*

and I have to apologise for the imperfect account of an occurrence which has much affected me, as it could not fail very much to affect any eye-witness.

I am, Gentlemen, your most obedient servant,

(Signed) ROBERT SINCLAIR.

As mentioned in the letter, the fireman was found dead under the engine, but the driver and the five passengers died later ; several other people were badly shaken and a few seriously hurt. The locomotive was a six-wheeled one, built by E. B. Wilson, of Leeds, in 1847, and had travelled approximately 270,000 miles ; it weighed in working order 23 t. 10 c. and had been generally repaired in October, 1859, the wheels then being turned up ; since then it had run about 10,700 further miles. The records of the Company were so badly kept that it was impossible to say who had made the wheels with which the engine was then running, although there was a possibility that Messrs. Stephenson's had done so, but no proof was forthcoming to support the contention. The origin of the tyres was also uncertain.

The accident was due to the failure of the tyre on the left-hand leading wheel, pieces of which were found some 160 " paces " (assumed to be yards) from the end of the platform. The driver was known to have sounded his tyres at Cambridge on the previous Saturday, but whether he did so on the morning of the accident—the Monday following—was not established. It was proved that the tyre which failed did so at the weld, which had a serious flaw in it ; there was also another flaw in the tyre, which seemed to be of inferior metal. The tyre had been shrunk on, but both the wheel and the tyre became deformed so that it was not making proper contact over the whole face. The moment the tyre failed at the weld it flew off the wheel and broke into several pieces. At the time the accident occurred the practice of fixing on tyres by means of some extra safety device, such as bolts or keys, was not in general vogue. The report on the accident dwells at some length on what was being done in this respect and stressed the absolute necessity of taking every precaution to ensure that a broken tyre would still remain reasonably well attached to the wheel. It appeared that Captain Tyler, who conducted the enquiry, had occasion previously to report on a similar accident—though fortunately less serious than the Tottenham one—which had happened on the London, Tilbury and Southend Railway to a train hauled by an E.C.R. locomotive. Here again in this case the Company were unable to supply any details or provide any record as to the history of the tyre that had failed and Captain Tyler said that the locomotive department of the E.C.R. appeared to be in very urgent need of re-organisation. Mr. Sinclair said he was doing his best towards that end.

Strong remarks were made at the enquiry on the poor braking power of the train, and it was suggested that it should have had another brake-van at the rear end (the only brake-van was next the engine and tender). The guard was looking out at the time of the derailment and acted very promptly in the emergency, but had a rear van been attached to the train it is quite possible that it might have had a strong steadying effect on the train as a whole, and thus diminished the serious consequences of the derailment. In any case Captain Tyler was of the opinion that it was obviously wrong to have only one brake-van running at the head of the train, as the application of the brakes merely helped to bunch up the train upon itself instead of keeping it pulled out from the engine ; this in many cases increased the tendency to derailment and might cause one where it would not otherwise occur.

At the final session of the inquest, held at Tottenham on the 16th March, 1860, and after hearing the lengthy evidence concerning the manufacture and performance of locomotive tyres, the jury came to the following verdict : '' We find that the deceased met their deaths from the breaking of the tyre of one of the leading wheels of the engine in consequence of the defective weld, and we are of the opinion that had proper caution and vigilance been used the same might have been detected.''

On the 3rd November, 1871, a rather curious accident occurred on the main line below the South Junction, but the staff of South Tottenham station were also involved. This station had been opened on the T. & H.R. after that line had been opened for some time and without itself, for some unexplained reason, having been inspected by the Board of Trade. It was then situated on a gradient of 1 in 100, falling towards the West Junction (the line through the existing station is level).

On the day in question the 8.6 a.m. Midland train from Kentish Town duly arrived at South Tottenham station, the train consisting of a tank engine, seven carriages and a guard's-van at each end. The engine was uncoupled and run round the train which was then pushed ahead until the engine was clear of the cross-over, duly reaching the up platform ready for the return journey. The guard had ridden in the rear van from Kentish Town, and on arrival announced that part of the brake gear and rigging on his van had fallen off, rendering the apparatus, if not useless, at least unreliable. The station-master on hearing this decided to shift the van to the other end of the train and not let it run in front in this unreliable state. He gave certain instructions regarding the securing of the wheels throughout the train to enable this to be done, but insufficient care was taken over it and the spragging came loose whilst the van was being uncoupled, for which purpose the engine set back slightly to facilitate disengaging the coupling hook. The train then commenced to run back down the grade, quite slowly at first, and an attempt was made to catch it up ; the station-master also ran along and tried to re-sprag a wheel or two, but to no avail. The train gathered speed towards the West Junction and then lost some of its impetus on the slightly rising grade to the South Junction. The signalman at the former gave a warning bell signal to the other man and both could observe what was happening.

It so happened that the South Junction home signals were off for the 8.15 a.m. train from Bishopsgate, consisting of a G.E.R. locomotive with eight coaches and two vans. It was approaching at about 35 m.p.h. and was about two hundred yards from the junction, according to the driver, when the home signal was thrown on. The driver acted promptly, reversed his engine, whistled for the brakes which were applied by the guards, and managed to all but stop the train when it struck the runaways, at a speed estimated at not more than 15 m.p.h. Some damage was done and people were shaken, but no vehicles were derailed.

Col. W. Yolland, who enquired into the accident, which had occurred at about 8.35 a.m., found that the station-master at South Tottenham—apparently a Midland Company's servant—had acted foolishly in not making sure that the spragging of the wheels of the train had been properly done. He should have seen that someone was there to hold a sprag rod or two whilst the van was being set back to free the coupling hook. In his opinion catch points should also have been provided on such an incline.

Before passing on to the next accident to occur within the Tottenham area, it will be as well to mention a letter which appeared in the *Tottenham Herald* for June, 1894. It is rather amusing and it is to a certain extent typical of the period. The document was from a local resident who complained of the overcrowding of the early morning trains. The writer had a particular grievance concerning the behaviour of a certain religious body of people who used the 6.19 a.m. train from Seven Sisters to Town. Apparently these fanatics, as he described them, passed the journey in singing, praying and preaching, and generally making themselves a nuisance to other passengers, and the writer wanted to know if they had the right to turn the train into a travelling mission hall. It should be remembered that in those days the third-class suburban coaches of the G.E.R. had the compartments open above the rack level, so that the occupants in any one compartment making themselves a nuisance affected the whole coach.

In 1911 there was the rather unusual occurrence of a petition to Parliament being presented by the local inhabitants concerning the alleged overcharges by the various railway companies concerned in the use of the Tottenham and Hampstead Junction Railway, especially the Great Eastern's traffic with the Great Northern and the London and North Western Railways and the complete ignoring of the T. & H. Act. A letter dated 2nd December, 1911, was directed to the Clerks of the Councils of Tottenham, Edmonton and other interested parishes in the Edmonton Union, pointing out the loss to the local ratepayers occasioned by the method of assessment for rates in respect of the T. & H.R. The writer showed how the difference between the gross assessment of £1,396 and the net one of £660, as concerning that portion of the railway within Tottenham, was 58 per cent., and enquired as to how the valuer had arrived at his calculation ; he had been unable to obtain the information anywhere. Another point made in the letter was that the South Tottenham goods yard was the sole property of the Midland Company, although access to the yard had to be over metals of the joint line. No trace could be found in the Council's books at the Tottenham Council's offices as to any payment by the Midland Company for rates regarding their own traffic at this yard. The letter went on to say that the rates in respect of the T. & H.R. were paid by the joint committee which received its revenue from a toll of the traffic passing over the railway, but the grievance of the writer was that some of the traffic was " toll free." An example of this class of traffic was that booked under a grouped rate as in the case of between London and Birmingham where certain rates for Bow and Kentish Town with Birmingham would be the same, although the mileage over the Tottenham and Hampstead and the intervening Great Eastern lines would be used without extra charge to the trader ; therefore, when this was done it was at the expense of the local ratepayers.

Returning to the list of major accidents, it was in the late evening on 29th August, 1913, that a collision occurred between two trains at the South Junction, as a result of which two passengers were badly injured and sixteen others slightly so. The trains involved were the 10.5 p.m. Spitalfields to Doncaster express freight and the 10.7 p.m. Liverpool Street to Great Yarmouth down passenger mail ; the latter train consisted of 4—4—0 locomotive No. 1888, its tender and seventeen vehicles. An enquiry into the accident was held by Lt.-Col. P. G. Von Donop, R.E.

The freight train had been brought to a stand at 10.13 p.m. at the South Junction home signal, and after a lapse of about six minutes it was run into at the rear by the 10.7 p.m. mail train from Liverpool Street. The freight brake-van was completely smashed and the engine of the mail slightly damaged, as were also two vehicles of that train.

At the enquiry the signalman at Clapton Junction box said that he received the " train out of section " signal from Copper Mill Junction box in respect of the freight train, and he then offered the mail train to the same box—this was at 10.15 p.m.— and as it was accepted he lowered his signals in the usual way ; a few minutes later the train passed his box. He mentioned that directly after lowering his signals he looked out of his cabin window in the direction of Hackney Downs and noticed that the back light of the Copper Mill Junction distant signal was showing, thereby indicating that the arm was in the *on* position at that moment, but when the train actually passed by him he was not able to see it owing to a quick increase in the fog which was gathering on the marshes at the time.

The signalman at Copper Mill Junction in his evidence said the freight train passed his box all in order, and that soon afterwards he was offered the mail train from Clapton Junction as mentioned in the previous paragraph. He accepted the train, but naturally did not offer it to Tottenham South Junction as he had not received the " train out of section " signal from that box in respect of the freight. He maintained that he did not lower his signals for the passage of the mail train, as indeed he could not, owing to their being electrically interlocked with the block instruments.

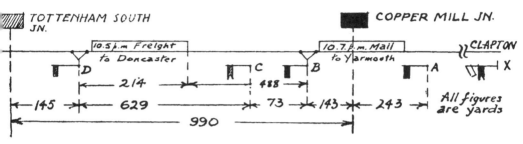

Diagram showing the positions of the two trains involved in the accident at Tottenham South Junction in August 1912. Signals " B " and " D " were provided with automatic detonator placing apparatus.

It is interesting to note here that one of the rules issued to signalmen was that if the weather became foggy and the fogmen had not arrived at their appointed stations, then during that period they should not accept a train from the box in the rear until they had received " train out of section " in respect of the preceding train from the box in advance. This rule was mentioned at the enquiry, as it was suggested that the signalman at Copper Mill Junction was in error in accepting the mail train whilst the section ahead was occupied by the freight train. The Inspecting Officer was not prepared to agree that the signalman at Copper Mill Junction was not justified in accepting the train as the weather was reasonably clear at the time, and the fog only became thicker directly afterwards. The driver of the mail train in giving evidence stated that he was positive that all signals from Clapton to Copper Mill Junction were clear for him to proceed but afterwards admitted that he did not see the two home signals (A and B on diagram), but still considered that as he saw the distant signal was off he might conclude that A and B were off also. He also insisted that he did not hear any detonators explode. The fireman drew his attention to a red light which he took to be the South Junction distant signal and he accordingly checked his speed, but suddenly the rear of the freight train came into view, too late however to prevent the collision. He estimated his speed at the time of the collision at about 6 m.p.h. ; the fireman confirmed the foregoing.

In his summing up, Lieut. Col. P. G. Von Donop pointed out that as there was a train in the section between Copper Mill and Tottenham South Junction the Sykes electric interlocking between the block instruments and the signals would prevent the Copper Mill Junction signalman from giving a clear road for the mail train. Thus he was of the opinion that in spite of the evidence of the driver and the fireman the mail train undoubtedly passed these signals whilst they were in the *on* position. As the driver admitted that he had not seen the home signals it was his duty to have brought his train to a stand until he had satisfied himself as to the position of these signals and to his whereabouts. Therefore, he had no alternative but to conclude that the accident was due entirely to the negligence of the driver of the mail train.

Before concluding the narrative of this accident it should be mentioned that from the evidence it was clear that some confusion arose over the fog signalling. Signal B was fitted with automatic detonator placing apparatus (the Great Eastern had many signals so fitted, especially advanced starting signals in the London area), and it is obvious that these detonators were exploded with the passing of the mail train ; the driver—if he did hear them—probably confused the explosion for fog signals at the Tottenham South Junction distant signal (C), as it should be remembered that he was not in a position to know that the fogmen had not then arrived at their respective posts. It would also suggest that the red light seen by the fireman was actually that of the Tottenham South Junction distant signal. (The reader will recall that in 1913 distant signals showed a red light when at caution, or danger as it was then called). Owing to the short distance—488 yards—between the signal B and the rear of the freight train it is clear that the mail train was on to it before the driver of the latter awoke to the danger of his position.

Mention must be made of the Lea Valley floods which, prior to the improvements in the river's channel, caused frequently much inconvenience to the railway and the surrounding districts. The number of times that flooding has occurred are too numerous to mention, but probably one of the worst occasions was in 1919, when between the 18th and 22nd of February matters were so serious as to suspend railway traffic for some time. The accompanying picture shows one of the floods, in the vicinity of the Hale Station, sometime prior to the first world war ; the viewpoint of this photograph is the exact opposite to that of the scene depicted in the frontispiece colour plate.

Up to the time of writing, the last serious accident involving a passenger train to take place within Tottenham, was a collision at the North Junction. This occurred at about eighteen minutes past five on the morning of 4th October, 1929, and by courtesy of Messrs. J. Dickinson & Co., of Basildon Works, South Tottenham, the writer is able to illustrate this particular disaster. The trains involved were the

5.5. a.m. Liverpool Street to Norwich express passenger and the 2.45 a.m. down freight from West Green to Churchbury (via Tottenham). The morning was very dark, but fine and clear.

The express was composed of twelve coaches with a tare of 234½ tons, being hauled by 4—6—0 locomotive No. 2808, *Gunton*. The freight train had fourteen empty coal wagons with a 20-ton brake-van, the locomotive in this case being an 0—6—0 No. 7938. Fortunately, from the casualty point of view, there were only seven passengers travelling in the express, and all subsequently complained of shock ; the driver and guard were also shaken, but were not prevented from attending to their duties afterwards.

The express locomotive was derailed after striking the wagons, but it managed to traverse a distance of some 140 yards before finally coming to rest at an angle of 45°. The leading coach following in the wake of the engine, left the rails and was severely damaged, but the other coaches remained on the rails and some of them were damaged also. The empty coal train was struck at the seventh wagon with a result that it and the preceding ones were completely smashed, but the engine, not being derailed, was pushed forward by the impact for a distance of some three hundred yards.

The empty wagon train had been brought to a stand at the North Junction home signal on the branch from the West Junction. It had remained in this position for at least ten minutes, when it moved forward on the main line ; the engine was running tender first. The North Junction home signal just referred to had four arms on the same post (it has since been replaced with a modern post with two arms only), as apart from the home arm there was also the Tottenham Station distant arm, a shunt signal and the West Junction distant arm. The driver of the empty wagon train stated at the enquiry that his reason for moving forward on to the main line was that he heard a sound close by him which resembled a dropping of a signal arm. He admitted that he did not actually see the arm move or the light change colour from red to green, but he was of the impression that when he looked up the top light on the post showed green. The North Junction signal-box is situated just north of the bridge carrying the Forest Gate line of the L.M.S.R. over the L.N.E.R. main line ; the centre of the cabin is thirteen yards from the tip of the junction points. When the engine of the empty wagon train was abreast of the cabin, the fireman drew the attention of his driver to the fact that the signalman was shouting at them from his window and displaying a red light. The driver stopped his train, but at the same moment the fireman saw the head-lights of the express approaching in the distance, and they both immediately jumped from their engine and scrambled clear ; directly afterwards the collision occurred.

The driver of the express, a man of some thirty-five years' experience, stated that he estimated his speed at about 45 m.p.h. when passing the South Junction. All signals, including the North Junction distant, were in the off position, but when the latter's home signal came into the driver's view around the slight curve, it was showing danger. He immediately closed his regulator, and made an emergency brake application, but it was quite obvious that nothing he could do would have prevented the collision. The fact that he applied the brake mitigated the results of the accident.

The North Junction signalman stated that the empty wagon train was offered to him from the West Junction at about a quarter of an hour before the express was due to pass, and after discussing the situation with the Tottenham station signalman decided to hold it at the branch home signal. The train duly came to rest, and he then dealt with an empty gas-tank train from the station to the West Junction. After this had passed by, he reset the roads for the main line and accepted the express from the South Junction box ; at the same time he accepted an up fast-fitted freight train from the station and offered it to the South Junction ; this passed through within three or four minutes, and it was immediately afterwards that the signalman heard the sound of his junction line points being forced. He rushed to his window, shouted to the driver and displayed a red light ; his next action was to throw all signals to danger and to send the obstruction danger signal to the South Junction box.

Lt.-Col. A. H. L.—now Sir Alan—Mount, who conducted the enquiry, concluded that he was at a loss to explain the empty wagon train driver's lapse from caution. Tests were subsequently made to repeat the noise the driver had alleged he had heard coming from the down branch home signal post, but nothing could be obtained to support his contention. It was recommended that a facing trap, or derailer, be provided on the down line of the branch just before the junction to prevent a train fouling the main line when the signals are against it.

Before concluding this chapter, mention must be made of a rather unusual accident which occurred on 7th January, 1931, at Northumberland Park. The 7.35 a.m. freight train from Temple Mills to Angel Road, hauled by 0—6—0 tender engine No. 7649, was " waiting clear " at Northumberland Park station with the light engine No. 7364 drawn up in the rear under the " permissive " rule (see signalling paragraph of previous chapter) when the 7.30 a.m. coal train from Victoria Park to Brimsdown, hauled by 0—6—0 locomotive No. 1265, ran into the back of the light engine, forcing it into the brake-van of the Angel Road train. Damage to this van was extensive and unfortunately the collision caused some petrol wagons, travelling next to the brake-van, to become ignited. The fire got out of control and destroyed the brake-van and also set fire to the coal in the bunker of No. 7364. The accident resulted in the death of the guard of the Angel Road train who was unfortunately burned to death in his van.

CHAPTER IV   Train Workings

FOR the purposes of this chapter the writer does not propose to enter into details of the history of individual locomotives, but rather to give a general review as to what now operates, and has operated, over the railways forming the subject matter of this book. Train working within the Tottenham area has always been very interesting and a large variety of steam locomotives have been, and still are, employed on practically every kind of traffic to be seen operating over British railways.

In pre-grouping days all types of Great Eastern and Midland engines were naturally much in evidence, but since 1923, and contrary to the general experience elsewhere, the variety of locomotives working in and through the district, especially during the latter years of the second world war, has considerably increased. One reason for this is the replacement, early in the war period, of the junction at Gospel Oak between the L.M.S.R. Camden Town–Willesden line and the end of the T. & H.R. ; this now enables Southern freight trains to work through from Feltham and other points on their system, to Temple Mills (Stratford). L.N.E.R. locomotives also work through to Willesden and beyond as well as special service and passenger trains of all three Companies.

On the main line one of the earliest types of locomotive to work over it was a little 2—2—2, built to the design of Robert Stephenson and was described by a writer of the period as follows :

" The engine is a six-wheel engine with the leading wheels, a small pair, just where those of other four or six-wheel engines are, behind the smoke-box. The driving wheels follow these, but are nearer the trailing wheels, and nearly under the centre of gravity of the engine. The trailing wheels are about 11 ft. from the leading, the same as other six-wheel engines, and instead of being behind the fire-box, as in six-wheel engines, are before it, a few inches nearer to it than are the driving wheels of four-wheel engines. The framing and bearings are all inside, as four-wheel engines are, and not as six. In short, in principle, it is almost a four-wheel engine lengthened in tubes fifty per cent., and placed on six wheels."

From a diagram of these engines it can be seen that they had exceptionally tall chimneys, with bell-shaped tops ; the boilers were devoid of any external fittings, and at the back of the domed fire-boxes there were provided open platforms for the drivers.

Ten years or so after the taking over of the Northern and Eastern by the Eastern Counties Company, we find that the main line train service consisted of six *down* trains, three of which called at Tottenham on week-days and Sundays ; two and one of these called at Marsh Lane respectively. In the *up* direction there were seven trains on week-days, none calling at Tottenham or Marsh Lane, but three connecting trains started from Broxbourne to serve, what was then, the outer suburban stations. There were three through trains on Sundays, two calling at Marsh Lane and Tottenham. All these services were augmented by the local Broxbourne and Hertford trains. A typical express train of the period, hauled by one of Sinclair's locomotives, is depicted in the coloured frontispiece.

Until the opening of the T. & H.R. in 1868, Tottenham station handled a very large traffic in cattle brought down from Norfolk and other parts of East Anglia for the London trade. This traffic was especially heavy at Christmas time, and to cope with the business Tottenham station was provided with an extensive cattle-dock on the *down* side of the line. Here again, the coloured frontispiece depicts the unloading of cattle at the long dock. With the opening of the G.E.R.'s own extensive cattle docks at Tufnell Park on the T. & H.R., much nearer to the great Metropolitan Cattle Market, situated just off the Caledonian Road, there was no longer the necessity for cattle to detrain at Tottenham.

From the formation of the G.E.R. in 1862 and right down to the grouping in 1923, practically every class of G.E. locomotive has worked through Tottenham at one time or another. When drivers and firemen did duties of twelve hours a day, or longer, as a matter of course, locomotives worked up to the London district from King's Lynn, Wisbech, Ely, Peterborough, and on occasions from as far away as Doncaster. Locomotives also worked through between Norwich and London (via Ely). Other sheds which worked their engines up to the Metropolis were Saffron Walden and, of course, Cambridge, so it will be seen that between all these depôts practically every class of engine on the system could be seen at different times passing along the Lea Valley. It should be remembered that some of these engines worked to and from St. Pancras as well as to Liverpool Street. With the introduction of the eight-hour day in 1912, these through workings from the more distant sheds were naturally curtailed and the only time their engines were seen in the London district was when they journeyed to Stratford for overhaul and repair.

MAIN LINE.

London, Cambridge, Norwich, and Yarmouth, with Wisbeach, Dereham,   Branches to Newmarket, Huntingdon, Peterborough, and Lowestoft.

DOWN TRAINS.	WEEK DAYS.								SUNDAYS.				FARES from London.

Distance from London	FROM	1 2 3 Class Mor.	Parl. 1 2 3 Class Mor.	1 2 Class Mor.	Exp. 1 2 Cl. Mail Mor.	1 2 3 Class Even	1 2 Class Even	1 2 Class Even	Mail 1 2 Class Even	1 2 3 Class Mor.	1 2 3 Class Mor.	Parl. 1 2 3 Class Even	Mail 1 2 Class Even
0	LONDON	..	6.15	10. 0	11.30	..	2.30	5. 0	8.40	..	7. 0	2. 0	8.40
1	Mile End	..	6.18	..	..	..	..	..	..	..	..	2. 3	..
3¼	Stratford	..	6.27	10.13	..	..	2.42	..	..	..	7.10	2.14	..
5	Lea Bridge	..	6.34	10.19	..	..	..	..	..	..	..	2.21	..
7¾	Tottenham	..	6.41	10.26	..	..	2.54	..	..	..	7.20	2.29	..
8½	Marsh Lane	..	6.45	10.31	..	..	..	..	..	..	..	2.34	..

A Market Train leaves Cambridge at 8.45 and Dereham at 9 a.m.   for Norwich, calling at all intermediate Stations, on Saturdays.

A pair of pages from Truscott's pocket time-tables dated 1854.

Some of the more important special Royal trains that passed through Tottenham have been described in the previous chapter. Apart from these very special trains, members of the Royal Family and their distinguished guests made frequent journeys between London and Sandringham, and in some cases between Windsor and Sandringham. Practically all the journeys which were not connected with Windsor started or terminated at St. Pancras.

Other special traffics that operated to or from St. Pancras were the Newmarket race specials, and both these and the Royal specials continued to do so until June, 1924, after which date they were transferred to King's Cross.

For many years St. Pancras had six booked G.E. trains in each direction ; four of these served Ely and Norwich, one to Hertford and the other to Tottenham. In latter years the traffic dwindled and with the great revision of Great Eastern time-tables in 1914, there remained only two through trains to Norwich, departing from St. Pancras at 12.22 and 5 p.m., the corresponding *up* trains arriving at 11.5 a.m. and 6.11 p.m. Besides these two trains there were a number of short runs to and from Tottenham to connect with the main line trains ; they usually consisted of two or three coaches that were attached to the *down* trains and slipped by the *up* ones. In latter years the slipping tended to decrease and *up* trains called at Tottenham. All these services were discontinued on 15th January, 1917, after which, only the special trains previously mentioned used St. Pancras. However, there was an attempt by the Great Eastern people to revive St. Pancras as their West End terminus in 1922, when a restaurant-car train was put on for Hunstanton. This train departed from the seaside town at 7.45 a.m. and returned back from St. Pancras at 11.50 a.m. It commenced to run on 24th July, 1922, but apparently did not pay as it was discontinued after that summer ; on the other hand, however, the grouping in 1923 may have had something to do with its withdrawal as the newly constituted L.N.E.R. were possessors of two West End termini.

It may be of interest to note that the L.N.E.R. still retains its powers to work into St. Pancras by way of the T. & H.R., but at the time of writing they are not exercised.

Bound up with the St. Pancras traffic are the stories of the Tottenham pilots. A pilot locomotive is one that is kept ready at important stations or junctions to take over in case of failures of train engines or to work specials at short notice. The St. Pancras pilot was stationed at Tottenham as being more convenient for traffic working purposes and also to avoid unnecessary rentals that would otherwise fall due to the Midland Company had the locomotives been stationed at St. Pancras. One of the earliest engines on this duty was a Sinclair 4—4—0 No. 327. In 1891, the Johnson 4—4—0 No. 306 went to Tottenham as pilot after having been at Wisbech and Braintree previously. This engine came to grief one day in 1897 on the Highgate Road bank and was subsequently withdrawn. Early in the present century there were two pilots stationed at Tottenham, one of them usually being a tank locomotive whose duties consisted of working forward the St. Pancras portions of the *up* expresses ; Nos. 1044 and 1049 were so employed when new. The tender engines were usually Nos. 497 or 498. The latter engine had the distinction of taking H.M. King Edward VII on his last rail journey on 2nd May, 1910. His Majesty had travelled up from Wolferton in a special saloon attached to an ordinary express bound for Liverpool Street, and as station pilot No. 498 worked the saloon forward to St. Pancras. The sad event of the King's death took place only four days later. After Nos. 497/8 went away to the country, the pilot stationed at Tottenham was generally one of the 1250-9 series.

In G.E. days the main line had the added interest of trial trips of locomotives fresh out from the Stratford shops. All locomotives that passed through the works, including new ones, ran light down to Broxbourne and back before passing into the paint shops or being handed over for traffic purposes. These light runnings were a daily occurrence—sometimes two or three engines a day—from Mondays to Fridays. Periodically, also, the little Worsdell four-cylinder tram-locomotives came up for overhaul from the Wisbech and Upwell Tramway.

The Cambridge main line has always carried more freight traffic than the Colchester one, chiefly on account of its direct connection with the agricultural district of the Fen Country and the mineral traffic from the South Yorkshire and Nottinghamshire coal fields. Fast freight trains, as well as coal trains, were worked up to Northumberland Park yard to be sorted out for the various G.E. suburban stations, and a considerable amount of sorting and marshalling is carried on at the Park yard. In recent years 2—8—0's of L.N.E.R., Classes 01 and 02 have worked the coal trains and the return empty trains, whilst during 1943-44 many U.S.A. and M.O.S. " Austerity " 2—8—0's and 2—10—0's worked over the Cambridge main line ; L.M.S.R. design 2—8—0's have also done turns over this route. Local freight trains, including those working on the Enfield and Palace Gates lines, were usually handled by 0—6—0's of L.N.E.R. Classes J14, J15, J16 and J17, and in recent years Classes J18, J19/1, J19/2 and J20 and the very fine Class J39. A few ex-G.N. 0—6—0's have worked in and about the Tottenham area in recent years and one of them can be seen in the photograph of the 1929 accident reproduced on page 36. During the heyday of the G.E.R. the heavy mineral traffic was worked by the E72 class 0—6—0's (Nos. 1240-9) and the 0—6—0 mineral engines of the 1150-1239 series.

Passenger expresses have been worked over a period of years by the standard express passenger engines of the day, including in later times, of course, the " Clauds " and the big 4—6—0's of the G.E. 1500 class.

When the 4—6—0 " Sandringhams " first appeared, several worked on the Cambridge main line, and two of them have carried the name *Tottenham Hotspur*. The first one was No. 2870, which carried the name for a few weeks when it was decided to streamline the locomotive for the newly introduced " East Anglian " expresses, and after the conversion the engine was renamed *City of London*. The name *Tottenham Hotspur* was afterwards given to No. 2830, formerly named *Thoresby Park*. No. 2870 was built by Robert Stephenson & Co. in May, 1937, and No. 2830 by the L.N.E.R. at their Darlington works in May, 1931. The renaming of No. 2830 took place in January, 1938.

The passenger train services on the main line now consist of expresses for Norwich (via Ely) and Hunstanton, local stopping trains for Bishop's Stortford and Cambridge, and the suburban Hertford trains. Most of the latter call at Tottenham, and in the case of the Bishop's Stortford trains where some of these are fast to or from Broxbourne, the Hertford trains make connections there for the other stations. All expresses, and some stopping trains, travel via Clapton and Hackney Downs, whilst others travel via Stratford to Liverpool Street. These latter are very useful for connections down the Colchester line or for stations on the Epping and Ongar routes.

So much for the main line, and from the few observations made it will be clear to the reader that a very large variety of interesting locomotives have passed along it during the one hundred odd years of its existence.

Of the Enfield and Palace Gates lines there is not a great deal to tell as the services have always been of the standard suburban variety and for many years trains were made up of four-wheel coaches, the third-class having wooden seats and with the compartments open above the rack level. Until about 1890 these trains were worked by the standard tank engine of the period, after which they were superseded by a class of small 0—6—0 tanks designed by James Holden and introduced originally for shunting duties and local freight working in 1886. Fifteen locomotives of this type were turned out in that year and were numbered 275 to 289 ; Nos. 290 to 304 were added in 1887. No. 294 from the last batch was fitted with the Westinghouse brake and tried out on the Enfield passenger service and proved very successful. This type of locomotive totalled eventually 240 machines, plus twenty smaller ones of similar design for branch work. These little locomotives were very successful and probably did as much hard and continuous work as any other class of locomotive in the country. They had the rather remarkable facility of being able to be reversed without stopping, and their general agility, coupled with the date of their arrival, quickly earned them the nick-name of " Jubilee Jumpers," which afterwards became " Buck Jumpers " and finally contracted to " Bucks." Eventually, they took over the whole of the Enfield and Palace Gates services, as well as the Chingford ones. The last batches of these locomotives that were built for passenger services were Nos. 51 to 60 and 81 to 90 of 1904 vintage ; Nos. 41 to 50 (of S.D. Holden's design) came out in 1912, all of which were slightly larger than their predecessors. A final ten were built in 1923, the first year of grouping, but received G.E. numbers 31 to 40.

In late 1911 a start was made by the Stratford works to convert the old four-wheel " bone shakers " into eight-wheel bogie stock and to improve the standard of comfort a little, and on 2nd March, 1913, a trial trip was made over the Enfield line with a train of these converts hauled by engine No. 43.

Just after the first world war the G.E.R. had to face the matter of electrification of their suburban lines, of which the Enfield route formed one of the principal arteries. Despite the obvious advantages of electric traction for suburban working, the Directors decided that an extensive reorganisation of their steam services would meet the needs of the travelling public, so in 1920 the world's most intensified steam-operated railway service came into being. Mention must be made of the unique scheme adopted to help passengers and operating staffs to distinguish the various trains. A coloured board was affixed to the sides of the guard's-van, of which for the Enfield line the hue was pale blue and for the Palace Gates trains, pink ; also, to facilitate station working, these trains had yellow and blue bands painted over the doors of the first and second class compartments respectively to help distinguish them from the third class compartments. The obvious nick-name of " Rainbows " was soon given to the trains by travelling Londoners.

Trains running through from Liverpool Street to Palace Gates alternated with two push-and-pull trains between Seven Sisters and Palace Gates. The first of these auto-trains were composed of two-coach sets worked by the " Crystal Palace " 2—4—2 tank locomotives, these being Nos. 1303 and 1305, No. 1304 being added later. For those unacquainted with the geography of London it might be as well to mention that Palace Gates Station is so named for its close proximity to the Alexandra Palace and that the nick-name " Crystal Palace " was given to the 2—4—2 tank engines, not because they worked into Palace Gates Station, but owing to their exceptionally large and well glazed cabs. Engine No. 1304 had been auto-fitted since 1915 to assist No. 1311 on the short-lived reopening of the Churchbury loop between Edmonton and Cheshunt.

Another feature of the train working that concerns Tottenham, is the fact that White Hart Lane was the terminal station of the auto-train service that operated over the Churchbury loop, Cheshunt being the other terminal point. It is not quite clear to the writer why White Hart Lane was chosen as the southern terminal for these trains as there was no special feature in the district to suggest its use as such. Edmonton (high level) would appear to have been the more appropriate station, or if it did seem necessary to extend the service up the London line, Seven Sisters Junction would surely have been more useful to passengers as the changing point.

In addition to the auto-trains and through Liverpool Street trains, the Palace Gates branch service was augmented by the through trains between the terminus and North Woolwich, travelling by way of South Tottenham and Stratford Market. With the opening of the curve between Seven Sisters and South Tottenham on 1st June, 1880, the first train services were between Palace Gates and Blackwall and later between Stratford and Palace Gates, but these were soon withdrawn. However, in 1887, the North Woolwich to Palace Gates service began to function and has remained

In being ever since, and, indeed, these are the only trains now running on the Palace Gates branch, with the exception of one through early morning train from Liverpool Street, which, incidentally, is the only train not calling at Stamford Hill. The auto-train service was withdrawn on 12th August, 1942. The Woolwich–Palace Gates trains run only mornings and evenings (mid-day Saturdays) with one train each way morning and evening on Sundays.

During the second world war the Enfield line services were standardised at half-hourly intervals during the slack period, and ten-minute intervals for the morning and evening busy periods.

After grouping, a link with the G.N. section was put in at Palace Gates, but this was only for stock exchanging purposes and could not be used for through running. About 1942, in an endeavour to relieve pressure on the main Cambridge and Peter-borough lines to London, coal trains were worked from New England to Temple Mills via Cuffley and Palace Gates, but owing to the nature of the lay-out at the latter place, some shunting was necessary there ; trains were usually broken into two parts to be worked forward to Temple Mills. Owing to the severe up grade from West Green to Seven Sisters, double heading by two 2—4—2 tanks was usual, or with lighter trains an 0—6—0 of Class J39 would function. In 1944, however, the Company took the necessary steps to rearrange the Palace Gates connection and now an ordinary double junction has been laid in at Bounds Green (Bowes Park) on the Cuffley–Hertford–Langley Junction line of the G.N. section. As a result of this, and on 12th July, 1944, through running was introduced between New England and Temple Mills, there being four booked trains each way daily ; these trains are limited to fifty wagons. The twists and turns and heavy grades of the route around central Tottenham, and the severe climb from West Green right up to Bowes Park makes this route a difficult one, but there is no doubt that the new junction at Palace Gates makes a very useful improvement. In the case of emergency it will now be possible to work passenger trains from off the G.N. section into Liverpool Street should King's Cross be out of action for any reason. As an example of this new advantage, a special fast freight train from Scotland was worked right through to Spitalfields via the G.N. main line, Cuffley, Palace Gates and Seven Sisters. The interesting point about this run was that the train used the direct route between Seven Sisters and Hackney Downs, via Stoke Newington, and this would appear to be the first time that a fast-fitted freight train from Scotland has worked over this line. This special trip took place in November, 1944. No doubt similar other special runs will be made by this way.

In recent years Stratford shops have been doing some repairs to G.N. section locomotives, chiefly 0—6—2 tanks of class N2, and also to coaching stock ; these proceed by way of the Palace Gates line and South Tottenham. Another occasional interesting working by this route is the turning of complete trains on the Tottenham triangle from off the G.N. section. When this is required to be done the train is brought down through South Tottenham and on to the main line beyond one of the junctions ; it is then reversed along the straight leg of the triangle and so back to Palace Gates. The ex-G.N. 0—6—0 saddle tank locomotives usually carry out this operation when necessary. A final note to conclude the activities of the Palace Gates and Enfield branches is to mention that the experimental L.N.E.R. 4—6—4 locomotive No. 10,000 went to the Norwich exhibition on 1st May, 1931, by means of the Bounds Green connection.

The working of the special football traffics to White Hart Lane have been described in the previous chapter, but it should be mentioned here that it was the general practice to work the special excursions for the Hotspur football matches from off the L.M.S.R. through to Northumberland Park.

In the early days of the T. & H.R. the passenger trains were worked by the Kirtley 0—4—4 tank locomotives Nos. 690–5 and 780–99, afterwards renumbered 1200–25. In 1875 the Johnson 0—4—4 tanks took over the working of the local passenger trains, a feature of these engines being the absence of cabs. Since the opening in 1868 there have been several changes in the train services, the first being provided by the G.E.R. between Fenchurch Street and Highgate Road. This was soon discontinued to be followed by the Midland service from Moorgate to Crouch Hill, extended to South Tottenham when that station was opened in 1871. Some years later the G.E.R. again ran a service over the joint line, this time from Chingford to Highgate Road and Gospel Oak.

In 1892 the G.E.R. started a service of their own from off the T. & H. line to Southend-on-Sea, via Stratford and Shenfield, probably in anticipation of the new service to Southend which would be available with the opening of the Forest Gate line, then being constructed. When this line was opened in 1894, a new train service was brought into being between St. Pancras, Barking and Southend. A regular service to Southend started in 1895 and was at first worked by Midland engines, but these were superseded by L.T. & S.R. locomotives in 1899. Special trains, however, continued to be worked by Midland locomotives. The beautiful Midland 4—4—0 locomotive No. 1757, *Beatrice*, was stationed at Shoeburyness for working these through Southend–St. Pancras expresses in company with a few other Midland engines ; upon their withdrawal in 1899 some L.T. & S.R. engines were stationed at Kentish Town. The first to go there was No. 5, *Plaistow*, followed by Nos. 4, 8, 10 and 28 (all of No. 1 class). They had to be fitted with the vacuum brake to work on Midland passenger stock. When the larger L.T. & S.R. locomotives (Class 2 intermediate), Nos. 43–48

GOSPEL OAK, HIGHGATE ROAD, WALTHAMSTOW, & CHINGFORD.—G.E. [Sundays.]

	mrn	mrn	mrn	mrn	aft	aft	aft	aft	aft	aft	aft	aft	aft	mrn	aft	aft	aft	aft	aft	aft	aft
Willesdn J.d	8 22	4 7 9	37	1052	1222	1	37	2 2 3	22 4	22 5	37 6	22 737	8	529	37	1037	8 35	...	9 55	1	30 2	30 330 430 530 630 730 830
Gospel Oak a	8 33	22 9	53	11 8	1238	1	53 2	38 3	38 4	53 5	38 753	9	8 9	53	1053	8 51	...	10 11	1	47 2	47 347 447 547 647 747 847
Gospel Oak dp	8 45	9 27	9 58	1123	1251	2	0 1	52 3	5 3 4	4 2 6	1 6	4 28	9 9	13 10	7 1055	9	559	63 12	1	51 2	51 351 451 551 651 751 [51]
Highgate Road	8 47	929	10 0	1125	1253	2	2 2	54 3	54 4	4 6	3 6	4 48	11	9 15	10 9	11	9	579	58 1253	1	53 2	53 353 453 553 653 753 853
Junction Road	8 49	931	10 2	1127	1255	2	4 2	56 3	57 4	4 8	5 6	4 68	13	9 17	10 11	11	2	59 9	57 1253	1	55 2	55 355 455 555 655 755 855
Upper Hollowy	8 51	933	10 4	1129	1257	2	6 2	58 3	59 4	4 8	7 6	4 88	15	9 19	10 13	11	4	1 9	59 1257	1	57 2	57 357 457 557 657 857
Hornsey Road	8 53	935	10 6	1131	1259	2	8 3	0 4	1 4	50 6	9 6	50 81	19	21	1015	11	69	3 10	1 1259	1	59 2	59 359 459 559 659 759 859
Crouch Hill	8 55	937	10 8	1133	1	1 2	10 3	2 4	3 4	52 6	11 6	52 819	9	21 1017	11	89	5 10	3	1 1	3	1 4 1 5 1 6 1 7 1 8 1 9 1
Haringay Park	8 58	940	1011	1136	1	4 2	13 3	5 4	6 4	55 6	14 6	55 822	9	26 1020	1111	9	8 10	6 1	4 2	4 3	4 4 4 5 4 6 4 7 4 8 4 9 4
St. Ann's Road	1	943	1014	1139	1	7 2	16 3	8 4	9 4	58 6	17 6	58 825	9	29 1023	1111	9	8 10	9 1	7 2	7 3	7 4 7 5 7 6 7 7 7 9 7
Sth. Tottenhm	9	3	946	1016	1141	1	9 2	18 3	10 4	11 5	0 6	19 7	0 827	9	31 1025	1111	6	13 1011	4	9 2	9 3	9 4 9 5 9 6 9 7 9 9 9 9
St.James's St	9 12	...	1022	1147	1	18 2	27 3	16 4	17 5	6 6	26 7	6 833	9	37	1031	1112	9	19 1017	1	15 2	15 3	15 415 516 615 715 815 915
Lea Bridge	9 27	...	1130	1239	1	35	...	3 27	4 23	5 24	...	7	21 9	1 9	59 1036	...	9	:6 1026	1	26 2	26 3	x8 426 526 626 726 826 938
Stratford ar	9 33	967	1138	1246	1	43	...	3 35	4 37	32	...	7	27 9	9 10	7 1036	...	9		1034	1	34 2	34 3	36 434 534 634 734 834 938
Hoe Street	9 14	...	1024	1149	1	17 2	29 3	18 4	19 5	8 6	28 7	8 835	9	39	...	1174	9	21 1019	1	17 1	17 3	17 417 517 617 717 817 917
Wood Street	9 17	...	1027	1151	1	20 2	22 3	21 4	22 5	11 6	32 7	11 838	9	42	...	1127	9	24 1022	1	20 3	20 3	20 420 520 620 720 820 920
Hale End	9 21	...	1031	1156	1	24 2	36 3	25 4	26 5	15 6	36 7	15 842	9	46	...	1131	9	28 1026	1	24 3	24 3	24 424 524 624 724 824 924
Chingford arr	9 25	...	1035	12 0	1	28 2	40 3	29 4	30 5	19 6	40 7	19 846	9	50	...	1135	9	32 1030	1	28 3	28 3	29 428 528 628 728 828 928
Chingford dep	8 52	10 0	1047	1232	1	48	0	...	3	44	40 6	0 7	18 8	18 9	10 1015	9	48	1248	1	48 2	52 3	48 44 5 548 48 52
Hale End	8 56	10 4	1051	1236	1	50	8	...	3	50	45 6	4 7	22 8	22 9	14 1019	9	52	1252	1	52 2	56 3	52 456 556 567 52 56
Wood Street	9	0	10 8	1055	1240	1	54 3	8	...	3	54	48 6	8 7	26 8	26 9	18 1022	9	56	1256	1	56 3	0 3	56 456 556 567 56 59
Hoe Street	9	3	1011	1058	1243	1	57 3	11	...	3	57 4	52 6	11 7	29 8	309	21 1026	9	59 1279	1	59 3	3 3	59 459 559 567 59 8 59
Stratford dp	740	8 35	...	1040	1153	...	2	38	330 3	38 4	38 5	46 6	30 5	14 9	12 1010	9	35	...	1	35 2	38 3	37 43 53 6 357 358 39
Lea Bridge	745	8 40	...	104	1158	...	2	43	3 43	43 5	9 6	3 48	209	17 1015	9	40	...	1	40 2	40 3	42 440 540 6 40 40 5 44
St.James's St	9	5	1012	11 0	1245	1	59 3	13	...	3	59 4	54 6	13 7	31 8	209	1015 9	40	...	1	3	5 4	1 5 1 6 1 7 1 8 1 9 1
Sth. Tottenhm	750	9	1012	11 0	1251	8	5 3	19	545 4	5 6	19 7	37 8	41 9	29 1034	10	7 1	7 2	7 3	11 4	7 5 7 6 7 7 8 7 9 7
St. Ann's Road	752	9	18	1021	11 8	1253	8	7 3	21	347 4	7 6	21 7	39 8	43 9	3 1036	10	9	9 2	9 3	11 4	9 9 8 9 9 9 9 9
Haringay Park	753	9	16	1021	1111	1256	2	103	23	310 4	10 5	6 24 7	42 8	46 9	7 1039	1012	1	12 3	12 3	16 4 1251	12 6	127 12 8 129 12
Crouch Hill	758	9	19	1027	1114	1259	2	13 3	27	353 4	13 5	8 27 7	45 8	49 9	37 1042	1015	1	15 2	15 3	15 4	1515 16 15 17	15 8 15 9 15
Hornsey Road	8	0	9 21	1029	1116	1	1 2	15 3	29	355 4	15 5	10 6	29 7	47 8	51 9	39 1044	1017	1	17 2	17 3	21 4	1517 617 17	17 8 17 9 17
Upper Hollowy	8	2	9 23	1031	1118	1	3 2	17 3	31	357 4	17 5	18 6	30 7	49 8	53 9	41 1048	1019	1	19 2	19 3	23 4	1919 619 19	19 8 19 9 19
Junction Road	8	4	9 26	1033	1120	1	5 2	19 3	33	359 4	19 5	14 6	33 7	51 8	55 9	43 1049	1021	1	21 2	21 3	25 4	21 521	621 7	21 8 21 9 21
Highgate Road	8	6	9 27	1035	1122	1	7 2	21 3	35	4 1 4	21 5	16 6	35 7	53 8	57 9	45 10 0	1023	1	23 2	23 3	27 4	23 523	623 7	23 8 23 9 23
Gospel Oak arr	8	8	9 29	10 7	1124	1	9 2	23 3	37	4 3 4	23 5	18 6	37 7	55 8	59 9	47 1052	1025	1	25 2	25 3	29 4	25 525	625 7	26 8 25 9 25
Gospel Oak d	814	9 44	1044	1129	1	42	29 3	44	4 44	29 5	06 7	59 9	149	59 10	26	...	1	34 2	34 3	34 4	34 534	634 7	538 34 539 53
Willesdn J.a	830	10 0	11 0	1149	1	30 2	49 4	0	433 4	49 5	49 7	2 8	19 9	30 1019	1119	...	1	53 2	50 3	534	53 553	653 7	538 53 9 53

[☞] For Stations between Willesden Junction and Gospel Oak, see pages 184 to 187.   * Walthamstow,

A reproduction of the page in the July, 1888, " Bradshaw's Guide " showing the first G.E.R.
train service from Chingford to Gospel Oak.

arrived in 1898, they took over the Midland workings from No. 1 class engines and remained almost exclusively on them. From 1905 onwards, these began to be rebuilt with larger boilers and were then transferred to Fenchurch Street duties ; afterwards, Nos. 51–68 usually worked into St. Pancras. Locomotives Nos. 37–48 were dual fitted when new.

In later years before the Midland purchased the L.T. & S.R. the only engine to be stationed at Kentish Town was No. 61, which became somewhat famous. In 1902 it was decorated elaborately for the Coronation of T.M. King Edward VII and Queen Alexandra. It was intended to allow the locomotive to work trains on Coronation Day, but owing to the sudden illness of the King the arrangements had to be postponed. However, the locomotive was put on show in the paintshop at Plaistow works for viewing by members of the staff and their families. Permanent adornments retained by this engine included a silver-plated cap to the chimney, copper stars mounted on aluminium on each cylinder head and also on the axle ends. A crown was painted on the side tanks underneath the name and above the coat-of-arms of the Company. The name of No. 61 was Kentish Town, the same as the shed at which it was stationed and where it remained for several years.

MIDLAND RAILWAY.—Between Tottenham, St. Pancras, Ludgate Hill, Moorgate Street, &c.

*** The Time Table not having arrived at the time of going to press, the Publisher cannot vouch for the correctness of these times.

DOWN TRAINS.

WEEK DAYS.

		B	B		C			AB		C		AB		Sat.	C				B		
Moorgate Street......	dep.	..	7 10	4 68	8 30	6 39	7 10	..	7 10	50 12	48 2	30 3	26 5	28 6	0 6	38 7	20 8	21			
Aldersgate Street ...	"	..	7 12	4 88	8 32	5 59	9 10	..	9 10	52 12	50 2	32 3	27 5	30 6	2 6	40 7	22 8	23			
Ludgate Hill	"	..	6 59	7 27	8 0	8 24	8 50	..	4 10	56 12	40 2	22 3	4 4	19 5	29	..	6 34	7 13 8	8			
Farringdon Street......	"	..	7 14	7 50	9 8	8 34	8 67	9	11 10	59 12	52 2	34 3	18 5	34 6	4 6	42 7	24 8	25			
King's Cross (Met.)	"	..	7 18	7 64	8 13	8 38	9	19	15 10	6 1	3 12	56 2	38 3	22 4	33 5	38 6	8 6	46 7	28 8	29		
St. Pancras...............	"	7 16	..	8	6	..	9	6			..	..	5	45			..		5	15		
Camden Road.........	arr.	7 19	7 23	7 69	8 18	8 43	9	6 9	20 10	20 11	..	8	1	12	43 3	27	38 5	44 6	13 6	17 6	33 8	34
Kentish Town.........	arr.	7 21	7 26	..	8	20	..	8			2 11	10	1			..			7	35		
	dep.	7 21	7 68	8	10	8 23	8 46	9		22 10	22 11	10	1	3 2	45 3	29	40 5	46 6	15 6	53 7	38 8	36
Highgate Road	"	7 24	..	..	8	26	8 48	..	9	25 10	25 11	13	1	6 2	48 3	32 4	4 5	49 6	18 6	56 7	41 8	39
Upper Holloway	"	7 27	8	2	..	8	29	8 50	..	9	28 10	28 11	16	1	9 2	51 3	35 4	6 5	52 6	21 6	59 7	44 8	42
Crouch Hill	"	7 30	8	6	..	8	32	8	53	..	9	31 10	31 11	19	1	12 2	54 3	38 4	9 5	55 6	24 7	2 7	47 8	45
South Tottenham	arr.	7 34	8	9	8	20	8	36	8	57	9	9	35 10	35 11	23	1	16 2	58 3	42 4	13 5	59 6	28 7	6 7	51 8	49

SUNDAYS.

		B	B	BO		B	B	B	
		7 57	9	20 1	12 1	26 5	11	..	
		7 59	9	22 1	14 2	28 5	13	..	
		..	9	4 1	4 2	4 5	4	..	
		..	9	24 1	16 2	30 5	16	..	
		8	5	9	28 1	20 2	34 5	19	..
		8	0	..		..		5	15
		3	14	9	33 1	25 2	39 5	24	
		..	9	35 1	27 2	41 5	26	..	
		8	16	9	39 1	31 2	45 5	30	
		8	19	9	42 1	34 2	48 5	33	
		8	22	9	45 1	37 2	51 5	36	
		8	25	9	48 1	40 2	54 5	39	
		8	29	9	52 1	44 2	58 5	43	

UP TRAINS.

WEEK DAYS.

		D	DEA		D	DE		DE		D	AD		D		Sat.		DE		DE	DE		D
South Tottenham......	dep.	7	44 8	13 8	28 8	46 9	9	27	0 11	49 1	40 1	40 3	22 6	23 6	14 6	34 7	12 8	9	
Crouch Hill	"	7	48 8	17 8	32 8	50 9	6	9	31 10	1 11	53 1	44 1	44 3	35 4	46 6	47 6	41 8	16 8	7	168
Upper Holloway	"	7	51 8	20 8	35 8	53 9	8	9	34 10	4 11	56 1	47 1	47 3	29 5	29 6	30 6	21 6	40 7	19 8	10
Highgate Road	"	7	54 8	23 8	38 8	56 9	11	9	37 10	10 11	59 1	50 1	50 3	32 5	32 6	33 6	24	..	7	22 8	13
Kentish Town.........	arr.	7	57	..	8	59 9	14	..	10	13	..	..	5	3				..	7	25 8	16
	dep.	3	8	26 8	41 9	3 9	17	9	40 10	14 11	18 12	21 1	57 3	34 5	35 6	30 6	27	..	7	25 8	16
Camden Road.........	"	6	8	29 8	43 9	5 9	19	9	42 10	16 11	20 12	41 5	57 3	37 5	37 6	36 6	32 6	40 7	18 8	20 8	10
St. Pancras...............	"	..	8	35	..	9	30	..	10	35	..	..	4	56			..	6	40	..	6	12
King's Cross (Met.)	"	..	8	34 8	48 9	10 9	24	9	47 10	21 12	25 12	4 3	14 4	25 5	28 6	47 7	0 7	27 8	21 8	33	..
Farringdon Street......	"	8	14 8	38 8	52 9	14 9	28	9	51 10	24 11	28 1	8 3	35 4	46 5	46 6	47 7	6 7	68 8	19 8	30	..
Ludgate Hill	"	8	21 8	41 9	..	9	21 9	30	10	0 10	30 11	38 1	12 3	58	..	2	123	58	..	6	47 7	10 8	..
Aldersgate Street ...	"	8	16 8	46 8	54 9	16 9	30	9	53 10	27 11	31 1	12 3	37 4	48 5	48 6	49 6	57 8	8 8	33 8	32	..
Moorgate Street.......	"	8	18 8	48 8	56 9	18 9	32	9	55 10	29 11	33 12	30	2	10 3	37 4	45 5	50 6	51 8	0 8	35 8	34	..

SUNDAYS.

		D	D		D	D	D		D	D	
		9	43 10	31	6 13	9	35 5	53		
		9	47 10	71	6 53	3	5 57	67		
		10	50 10	10 1	6 53	1 66	6	0	
		9	53 10	13 2	13 3	96	5	36	3
		9	56 10	16 2	4 3	22	6	6	
		9	59 10	19 2	7 3	25 6	86	10	
		1 10	21 2	9 3	27 6	8 12	6	12	
		..	..		6	12	
		6	10	10 30	2	14 8	33	..	6	17
		10	10 10	30 2	18 3	36	..	6	21
		36 10	5 12	37 3	66	..	6	36
		6	88 10	61 2	20 3	88	..	6	23
		14 10	34 2	22 3	40	..	6	25

A.—Passengers to or from Ludgate Hill and L. O. and D Line, by Trains marked A, do not change Carriages; by Trains they change at Farringdon Street.

B.—Passengers from Moorgate Street for Tottenham and Hampstead Line, by Trains marked B, change Carriages at Kentish Town.

C.—Passengers from St. Pancras for Tottenham and Hampstead Line, by Trains marked C, change Carriages at Kentish Town.

D.—Passengers from Tottenham and Hampstead Line for Moorgate Street, by Trains marked D, change Carriages at Kentish Town.

E.—Passengers from Tottenham and Hampstead Line for St. Pancras, by Trains marked E, change Carriages at Kentish Town.

The first time-table for the T. & H.R. upon the opening of South Tottenham station, May, 1871.

In passing it is interesting to note that very few Midland locomotives had the distinction of being named, as was the case of those belonging to the Great Eastern ; therefore, it was somewhat remarkable that *Beatrice* and *Petrolea*, the G.E. 2—4—0 oil burning engine No. 760, both worked over the T. & H.R. Thus, it probably happened that they were to be seen side by side, perhaps at South Tottenham, and they must have made a splendid contrast in their distinctive liveries of crimson lake and royal blue respectively.

When the Midland started using their running powers over the G.E. main line down to the Thames Docks, some 0—6—0 tender locomotives were used ; these were Kirtley's well-known double-framed machines of the series 360–79. In 1871, Beyer, Peacock & Co. delivered ten 0—6—0 side tank engines ; these were numbered 880–9, and as in the case of the 0—4—4 tanks they were without cabs. They were later reboilered and renumbered 1610–9.

Since the opening of the Forest Gate line, the Midland, and since 1923, the L.M.S.R., have maintained a regular suburban passenger train service between St. Pancras (or Kentish Town) and Barking, with a few trains to or from East Ham. Originally, the service was a good one but it has tended to diminish gradually, and since the grouping it can really be called poor and, during the winter of 1944, extremely bad. There have always been through trains between St. Pancras and Southend, which were reduced to two each way daily (with extras on summer Sundays) during the second world war ; the 1944 D-Day cuts saw the departure of one of these, thus leaving only one through train. With the coming of peace in Europe in May, 1945, the L.M.S.R. were quick to restore the through St. Pancras–Southend trains so as to afford North Londoners better facilities for getting to the sea for a well-earned rest and holiday. During August and September there were five through trains each way and evidence as to the way the public took advantage of these additional trains can be gleaned from the fact that 58,634 passengers booked from South Tottenham* to Benfleet, and stations beyond, during the three months of July, August and September.

In peace-time special boat trains are run between St. Pancras and Tilbury Docks, as well as many excursions to Southend, including some from off the old Midland section main line. The focal point of traffic on the T. & H.R. is, of course, South Tottenham, and the five chains stretch through the station, which separates the two junctions, has always carried a traffic that can rightly be described as concentrated. As an example of the intensity of this traffic the passenger train service of the summer of 1914 can be quoted ; this comprised no fewer than 119 Midland and 70 Great Eastern trains. This was the *ordinary* passenger service and to it must be added the excursions, boat trains, Great Eastern expresses from St. Pancras and freight traffic. The latter has always been very heavy when it must be remembered that the Midland

*The corresponding figures for Harringay Park were 40,452

and Great Eastern, and their successors the L.N.E.R. and L.M.S.R. work many regular freight services through the Tottenham area. During the winter of 1944, when the passenger trains (if not the traffic) can be said to have touched a low record, forty-three L.M.S.R. and twenty-six L.N.E.R. passenger trains called at South Tottenham on week-days (Mondays to Fridays), but it must be remembered that the freight traffic and special service trains increased considerably. Heavy oil tank trains, both empty and full, made frequent use of the T. & H.R. line on their journeys to or from the Thames-side loading points.

*   *   *

To conclude this chapter, and to indicate the variety of locomotives that work through and around about the Tottenham district, the writer gives the following list of engines that he himself observed during the summer of 1944.

L.N.E.R. : 4—6—0's of B12/3 and B17 classes ; 4—4—0's of classes D16 and D16/3 ; ex-G.N. 2—6—0's, class V1 2—6—2T ; 0—6—0's of classes J14, J15, J16, J17, J18, J19/1, J19/2, J20 and J39 ; 0—6—0 tanks of all ex-G.E. classes ; ex-G.N. 0—6—0ST ; 0—6—2 tanks of classes N2 and N7 ; 2—8—0's of classes O1 and O2 ; ex-G.E. 2—4—2 tanks (all classes).

L.M.S.R. : Standard 0—6—0T ; 2—6—2 and 2—6—4 tanks of both Fowler and Stanier designs ; ex-L.T.S. 4—4—2 tanks, classes 2P and 3P ; 2—6—0 (Fowler) ; 2—8—0 (including those built under W.D. contract) ; standard 0—8—0 (class 7F) and 0—6—0 (class 4F) ; Stanier 4—6—0's of both 5P and 5XP ; ex-Midland 0—6—0's and 0—4—4T (class 1P) ; 4—4—0 class 2P, 3P and Deeley compounds.

S.R. : 0—6—0's of classes C and Q1.

M.O.S. and U.S.A. : 2—8—0's.

Some M.O.S. 2—10—0's commenced working up and down the main line between Temple Mills and March early in 1945.

CHAPTER V   Some Closing Notes

I N the previous chapter the writer outlined the train services operating in and around Tottenham, and during the present century there has been little change in the make-up of local time-tables, excepting that there has been a steady decline in the frequency of the trains over most of the routes. It is unlikely now that there will be much change, unless further steam trains are withdrawn, until some drastic change in the whole situation takes place, such as electrification of the lines concerned.

It seems almost a certainty that electrification of the late Great Eastern suburban lines will come about, and perhaps also the T. & H.R. It is interesting to note that at the time of writing the electrification of the Enfield and Churchbury-loop lines has the urgent support of the local authorities. In 1944 a deputation of Mayors and Town Clerks from the boroughs concerned attended the officials of the L.N.E.R. to urge upon them the necessity of electrifying the lines in question, including the re-opening of the Churchbury loop. Having regard to the electrification of some of the other L.N.E.R. suburban lines, it is rather obscure as to how the desired change-over will be effected, especially in view of the rather unusual nature of the train services involved.

In the case of the T. & H.R. and the Forest Gate line of the L.M.S.R., the indication is for an extension of the latter's London suburban electrified system from Gospel Oak to Barking thus linking up with the District trains to Upminster. By running around the eastern leg of the East Ham triangle a new " Outer Circle " could be established by way of Willesden, Gospel Oak, Tottenham, East Ham, the District line, Earls Court, Addison Road to Willesden. One drawback to this scheme would be that the service could not contact Kentish Town for connections on the old Midland main line, unless the short section between Junction Road and Kentish Town be electrified also. Alternatively, the Forest Gate line traffic might stand three or four through steam trains each way daily from Southend-on-Sea to St. Pancras ; these trains would be sufficient to supply connections at Kentish Town for stations on the main line north thereof. In any case it would be desirable to retain some through Southend trains as this has been a facility that has always been enjoyed by Tottenham residents.

For the L.N.E.R. lines it remains to be seen whether the services will be worked by that Company themselves in conjunction with their own electrification scheme out to Shenfield, etc., or whether the railways become surface extensions of the L.P.T.B. underground system as has been done with the Barnet, Edgware and Alexandra Palace branches, and the partly developed scheme for the Ongar and Fairlop lines.

To comprise a comprehensive public service, the electrification should extend out to Hertford, as well as Enfield Town and Palace Gates. In the case of the two latter branches the train services should be so arranged as to interlink at Seven Sisters, giving regular connections each way, say quarter-hourly for London and Enfield and half-hourly for Palace Gates and Woolwich.

The writer can foresee that the railway companies will at once raise the objection that as the T. & H. R. carries such an intensive freight traffic, a closely worked passenger service would be impracticable, but it should be possible to arrange the time-table so that all the four trains (the Woolwich-Palace Gates and Barking–Willesden trains) each half-hour at South Tottenham could pass through within a space of six to eight minutes, thus giving a twenty-two-minute clearance for other traffic. This would also have the advantage of providing regular connections between the places mentioned in the brackets. Further, this electrification should not interfere with the special boat expresses that the L.M.S.R. has to provide for the Tilbury steamships. The railways would indeed be making out a poor case for themselves if it had to be admitted that an adequate passenger service is not possible owing to the cumbersome working of freight traffic. It must be admitted that at the present time the normal winter passenger traffic on the T. & H. and Forest Gate lines is very light, but from conversations with local residents and personal observation by the writer, this would appear to be entirely due to the existing poor steam train services.

The existing half-hourly steam service on the Enfield line is excellent and good time is generally kept ; this gives a direct service from Tottenham to Bush Hill Park and Enfield. The trains are reasonably well patronised, but there is no doubt that a regular tube train service would be used to its full capacity.

It would appear that with electrification the Tottenham railways will have a revival, but with the improvement in the train service it will be necessary to rebuild and modernise the stations. In the case of White Hart Lane, Bruce Grove, West Green and Harringay Park, the stations are well situated and call for no alteration other than the improvement of their approaches, waiting rooms and other amenities. The Hale and Northumberland Park stations are also well situated, both for serving factory colonies and residential areas, but need drastic rebuilding and modernisation to bring them into line for present-day needs. Plans were ready for rebuilding Tottenham station in 1939, but the outbreak of hostilities caused the work to be postponed.

A major improvement that would be of undoubted value to the public and probably of some economic benefit also to the Companies concerned would be the building of an entirely new station in South Tottenham to take the place of Seven Sisters Junction, South Tottenham and the already closed St. Ann's Road stations. The new arrangement would be one large exchange station erected on that spare back land where the Enfield line crosses over the T. & H.R. A suitable name for the new station would be South Tottenham Junction.

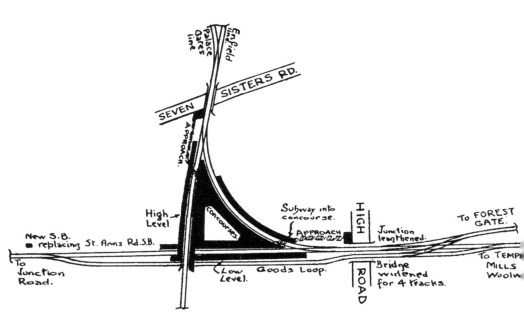

The Author's suggested scheme for a new junction station to replace the three existing stations of Seven Sisters Junction, South Tottenham Junction, and St. Ann's Road. (Closed). The arrangement also provides for freight running loops and an improvement in the alinement of South Tottenham Junction between the T. & H.R. and the Forest Gate line of the L.M.S.R.

The accompanying plan will show the advantage of such a scheme, but to appreciate the full effects of the improvement it will be as well to point out the disadvantages of the two existing stations. The South Tottenham one is fairly well situated from the public's point of view, but as the station is confined to a length of nine chains between the two junctions, the platform length is restricted. The open approaches to the platforms are another serious defect. Apart from the short platforms, the sharp turnout for the Forest Gate line necessitates a reduction of speed for through trains to or from that line, which is a serious handicap for those west bound.

At Seven Sisters, the Palace Gates line suffers from the long walk necessary to reach the platforms from the main booking office in West Green Road. To help those passengers who live on the Seven Sisters Road side of the station, a small booking-office is available ; this, however, is now open only in the early mornings and when it is closed persons on that side of the station wishing to travel to Palace Gates, etc., have to walk right round the station site, a considerable distance, book a ticket and then make their way back to the platform by way of the long footpath described in chapter II. The distance of the Palace Gates line platforms from the main roads and main booking office is undoubtedly an adverse factor in respect of the passenger traffic on the branch and probably led to the withdrawal of the auto-service in 1942.

The combining of Seven Sisters and South Tottenham stations would offset some of these disadvantages, and passengers using the latter station regularly would not be inconvenienced in any way by the situation of the new junction. One entrance to it would be in the High Road exactly opposite to the existing station entrance. The approach would be by means of a broad and well illuminated covered way that would run along the north side of the existing embankment for about fifty yards or so and then pass under the South Tottenham–Seven Sisters curve to enter a spacious concourse and booking-hall situated in the apex of the angle between the two railways. The new station itself would consist of six platforms : Nos. 1 and 2 being on the T. & H. line with Nos. 3 and 4 on the Enfield line ; Nos. 5 and 6 would be situated on the curve. Nos. 1 to 4 would connect at the point where the Enfield line crosses over the T. & H.R. and stairways would be provided to enable passengers to change trains without undue walking. The scheme provides for a second booking-hall in the north point of the triangle, with an exit and entrance into the Seven Sisters Road. Both entrances would make contacts with several trolley-bus routes, and in this respect would undoubtedly relieve the pressure at the Manor House station on the Piccadilly line, a matter which the L.P.T.B. will agree is somewhat necessary.

A small number of lock-up shops and kiosks could be erected in the concourse and approaches, which would not only add to the railway company's revenue, but also add to the cheerfulness and general usefulness of the station. With the completion of the new exchange junction, three important suburban passenger services would be interlinked and brought under the control of one station-master and his staff.

At the time of writing the land is available for the development of this scheme and is actually lying idle, except for its use as garden allotments, and no engineering difficulties should be experienced in the work. One great advantage from the railway viewpoint and one that should interest the operating department, is the fact that the Forest Gate Junction could be lengthened out for fast running, and also a double running loop of nearly one mile in length could be constructed ; the latter would help considerably the working of the intensive freight traffic on the T. & H.R. The plan shows how these alterations could be effected.

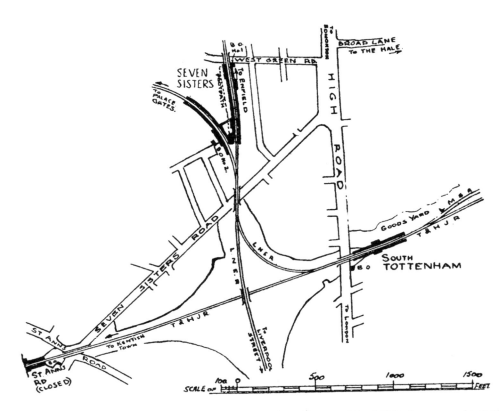

Sketch plan of the existing lay-out of the stations in the Seven Sisters and South Tottenham areas showing their positions in relation to the main roads.

Whether the foregoing ideas will ever take practical shape, only the future will show, and it will be interesting to see how things work out in the next decade. The railways have now reached a point in their history when drastic overhaul is needed and bold action in this respect will surely lead to future prosperity. Should such action take place another chapter will be necessary to complete this book, if and when a second edition ever becomes a necessity to the railway enthusiasts' library.

APPENDIX A

Some notes on the Tottenham and District Gas Company's Internal Transport System

The Tottenham and District Gas Company has, from a small beginning in 1847, developed into one of the leading gas undertakings of the United Kingdom, and with its subsidiary companies, now serves a large area of north and north-east Middlesex, Hertfordshire and parts of Bedfordshire.

The principal and largest of the company's works are situated just inside Edmonton, the boundary between Tottenham and Edmonton forming the southern extremity of the works ; they are adjacent to the L.N.E.R. main line, and a system of internal sidings serving the works is connected therewith by a facing siding off the down fast road at Northumberland Park (see map on page 30) and a trailing connection near Angel Road station. All the coal for the works is brought by rail and two types of wagons are necessary, end opening and ordinary. Complete trains of the former type work down from the Yorkshire coalfields by way of Doncaster and through to Northumberland Park yard, from whence they are transferred to the works. The wagons are emptied by hydraulic tipping rams between the rails which engage the axle remote from the end door and elevate that end until the floor of the wagon is at angle of about 50° with the horizontal.

The ordinary wagons are used to convey coal from the London docks as this coal comes down from Co. Durham by coastal vessels. These wagons are unloaded by a rotary tipper. The Company is the owner of a considerable number of ten-ton open wagons, which, in normal times, operate regularly between the works and the coalfields. The amount of coal entering the works every year averages 250,000 tons, which is quite a respectable amount of traffic.

The first locomotive to be employed in the Company's works was a Peckett 0—4—0ST of 1895, the maker's number being 631, the boiler having a pressure of 140 lbs. p.s.i. ; it was scrapped in March, 1930. A similar engine, No. 2, started work in 1904, the maker's number being 1027, but this had a boiler working at 150 lbs. pressure and served until April, 1931. No. 3, also an 0—4—0ST, from the Falcon Engine Co., had a boiler pressure of 120 lbs. This was purchased second-hand in 1924 and was scrapped in June, 1935.

A fully equipped workshop, capable of building small locomotives, as well as carrying out normal repairs required by the various units of the Company's transport system, is available at the Tottenham works and locomotive No. 4 was built here in 1925. It was originally an 0—4—0 chain-driven (from a Garratt steam wagon) and had a boiler working at 200 lbs. pressure. In 1937 it was converted to a petrol-electric locomotive on the Dennis-Stevens principle. It is fitted with 30 in. diameter wheels and as now constructed will haul six loaded standard coal wagons.

Locomotive No. 5 is an 0—4—0 Sentinel, gear and chain driven, built in 1929, starting at the works in January, 1930. The maker's number is 8087, and it has two vertical cylinders $6\frac{3}{4}$ by 9 in. stroke, supplied with steam from a boiler working at 275 lbs. p.s.i. pressure. The weight in working order is 17 tons and the tractive effort at 85 per cent., 11,000 lbs.

The next locomotive, No. 6, is another product of the home works and is an 0—4—0 chain driven machine converted from a Sentinel steam wagon engine and boiler. It started work in March, 1935, and has the following dimensions ; two horizontal cylinders, 6¾ by 9 in. (stroke) ; 24 in. diameter wheels ; boiler pressure of 230 lbs. p.s.i. ; weight in working order, 12 tons and a tractive effort of 9,000 lbs. No. 7 on the Company's books is an 0—4—0 chain-driven Sentinel, which also started work in 1935, and is similar in all respects to No. 5.

Nos. 8 and 9 were both built in the shops at the Tottenham works. They are petrol driven with the 0—4—0 wheel arrangement. No. 8 has a 24 h.p. engine and will haul four loaded wagons at 4 m.p.h., whilst No. 9 uses a 14 h.p. Morris engine and will move two wagons at 2 m.p.h. The former is on duty at the Hertford works and the latter at the Southgate works, starting in 1938.

Finally, No. 10, is an 0—4—0 steam, gear and chain driven. It was built by Atkinson, Walker, their classification being No. 113, " Class C." It is fitted with 27 in. wheels and the boiler carries a pressure of 230 lbs. p.s.i. The weight in working order is 10 tons ; it was rebuilt in January, 1943.

The locomotives at the Tottenham works are employed in shunting the loaded wagons in and out of the various parts of the works after they have been delivered by the L.N.E.R. to the reception sidings, and also in making up empty wagon trains for their return to the collieries.

APPENDIX B

Signal Boxes

	Situation	Present Railway	Railway pre-1923	Number Levers	Block System	Remarks
1	Northumberland Park	L.N.E.	G.E.	46	Sykes' lock and block	Level crossing
2	Tottenham	L.N.E.	G.E.	46	Ditto	Does not control slow roads
3	North Junction	T. & H.	G.E.	62	Sykes' lock and block for main line ; Tyer's block telegraph to West Junction	Ditto
4	South Junction	L.N.E.	G.E.	31	Ditto	Ditto
5	West Junction	L.N.E.	G.E.	20	Tyer's block telegraph to North and South Junctions ; Midland single needle to South Tottenham Junction	Also controls entrance to South Tottenham goods yard
6	South Tottenham Junction	L.N.E.	G.E.	50	Midland single needle for T. & H. line ; Tyer's block telegraph to Seven Sisters Junction ; Midland rotary block for Forest Gate line	
		T. & H.	T. & H.			
		L.M.S.	Midland			
7	St. Ann's Road	T. & H.	T. & H.	10	Midland single needle	
8	Harringay Park	T. & H.	T. & H.	15	Ditto	
9	Seven Sisters Junction	L.N.E.	G.E.	47	Three Westinghouse illuminated diagrams for Enfield, Hackney Downs, and junctions sections. Sykes' lock and block for junction signals. Tyer's block telegraph to West Green and South Tottenham	Also controls ground frame for entrance to Town Hall sidings
10	West Green	L.N.E.	G.E.	20	Tyer's block telegraph	Closed 2nd September,1934
11	Bruce Grove*	—	G.E.	—		Closed 2nd September, 1934, also has two ground frames for goods yard controlled by Seven Sisters and Edmonton Junction boxes
12	White Hart Lane	—	G.E.	—		

*The same details apply to Stamford Hill.

(Above) *An example of the serious flooding caused by the River Lea overflowing in the winter time. The view is just south of Tottenham station. (From a lantern slide kindly lent by W. A. Bennett (Tottenham Borough Librarian).*

(Below) *G.E.R. 2-4-2 locomotive No. 1304 Palace Gates—Seven Sisters auto-train service standing in Seven Sisters station (circa 1922). From the Author's collection.*

(Above) *St. Ann's Road station (now closed) looking towards South Tottenham.*

(Below) *White Hart Lane station looking northwards.*

(Above) *Looking westwards from South Tottenham junction showing the T. & H. R. and the L.N.E.R. line to Seven Sisters Junction diverging to right. The Hackney Downs—Edmonton line can be seen in middle distance crossing over the T. & H.R.*

(Below) *Bruce Grove station looking northwards.*

A group of six G.E.R. tickets associated with the Tottenham district. The top left hand one shows a single 3rd-class issued to Park (now Northumberland Park). The centre left-hand one is a specimen of the ticket issued on the T. & H. R. and is headed T. & H. Ry., Mid. & G.E.J.C. (Tottenham & Hampstead Railway Midland & Great Eastern Joint Committee). The lower right-hand one shows an early specimen of a " Parliamentary Third Class " issued between Seven Sisters and Stamford Hill just after the opening of the line (The reproductions are a little over full size).

Date	Situation	Cause	Damage
11/1/41	Near White Hart Lane Station, west side of line opposite goods yard	Two H.E. bombs	Damage to embankment
17/1/41	Between Belmont Avenue and Westbury Avenue, Palace-Gates line	Unexploded A.A. shell	Slight damage to track
14/3/44	West Green Station	A.A. Shell	Damage to up platform
21/3/44	Near Tottenham Station	Incendiary bombs	Fogman's hut destroyed
21/8/44	Cornwall Road	Flying bomb	West Green down home signal ; spectacles broken

ERRATA and ADDENDA

The initials of Mr. Bennett, the Borough of Tottenham Librarian, should read W. J. Mr. Bennett has retired since this book went to press.

Chapter 2. **Diagram of Northumberland Park Station.** The signal arm controlling the entrance to the Gas Work's sidings is not a scissors pattern as indicated, but a small ordinary lower quadrant arm. The scissors arm is on the extreme right and refers to the slow road.

Chapter 3. **Tottenham South Junction accident.** The date of the year referred to should read 1913, not 1912.

The distance between the two junctions at South Tottenham is given as five chains and nine chains on different pages. The latter figure is the correct one, the one of five chains being the actual platform length of the station.

Drawing of Locomotive 2830. The artist has shown the style of lettering wrongly for this particular locomotive, as the author understands that No. 2830 always carried her number on the cab sides.

Appendix C, second column, bottom line. The initials should read L.P.T.B. (London Passenger Transport Board). This section of the Piccadilly Tube was opened to traffic on 19th September 1932.

Detailed Map of the surface railways within the Borough of Tottenham. The distances indicated are miles and decimals of a mile.

To Silver Street Stn. Box

.875

Station Box (Closed)

WHITE HART LANE

.7875

To Noel Park & Wood Green Stn. Box

.9375

Station Box (Closed)

BRUCE GROVE

Stn Box

WEST GREEN

.825

Private

.8875

SEVEN SISTERS

Junc. Box

.275

1.58 To Black Horse Road

HARRINGAY PARK

ST. ANN'S ROAD

.3875

STH. TOTTENHAM

.4

—.8625—

—.425—

Stn. Box (Closed)

Stn Box

Stn. Box

Stn. Box

STAMFORD HILL

.6125

—.725 To Crouch Hill

To Stoke Newington Stn. Box

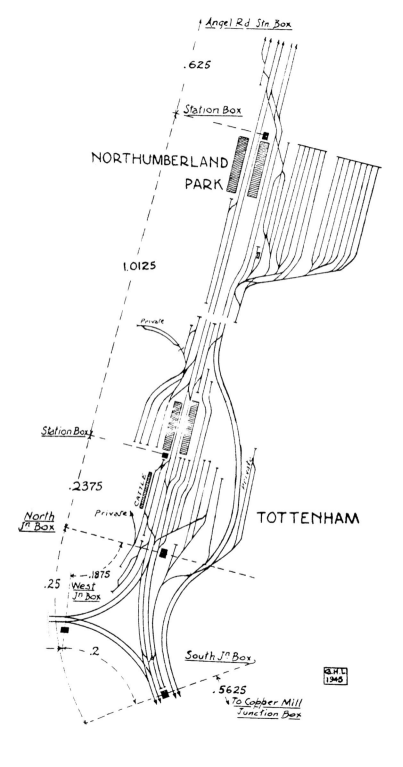

Angel Rd Stn Box

.625

Station Box

NORTHUMBERLAND
PARK

1.0125

Private

Station Box

.2375

North
Jⁿ Box

Private

CATTLE

Private

TOTTENHAM

.25

West
Jⁿ Box

.1875

.2

South Jⁿ Box

.5625

To Copper Mill
Junction Box

G.H.L
1945